A Color-Blind Church

Integration Under the Steeple

David E. Leininger

CSS Publishing Company, Inc., Lima, Ohio

THE COLOR-BLIND CHURCH

Copyright © 2007 by
CSS Publishing Company, Inc.
Lima, Ohio

All rights reserved. No part of this publication may be reproduced in any manner whatsoever without the prior permission of the publisher, except in the case of brief quotations embodied in critical articles and reviews. Inquiries should be addressed to: Permissions, CSS Publishing Company, Inc., 517 South Main Street, Lima, Ohio 45804.

Some scripture quotations are from the Revised Standard Version of the Bible, copyrighted 1946, 1952 ©, 1971, 1973 by the Division of Christian Education of the National Council of the Churches of Christ in the USA. Used by permission.

Some scripture quotations are from the Holy Bible, New International Version. Copyright © 1973, 1978, 1984 International Bible Society. Used by permission of Zondervan Bible Publishers. All rights reserved.

Library of Congress Cataloging-in-Publication Data

Leininger, David E., 1944-
   Color-blind church : integration under the steeple / David E. Leininger.
   p. cm.
   Includes bibliographical references.
   ISBN 0-7880-2439-6 (perfect bound : alk. paper)
  1. Liberty Hill (S. C.)—Church history. 2. Liberty Hill (S.C)—Race relations. 3. Presbyterian Church (U.S.A.)—History—20th century. 4. Race relations—Religious aspects—Presbyterian Church (U.S.A.) 5. United States—Race relations. I. Title.

BX8949.L53L45 2007
285'.175761—dc22

2006028229

For more information about CSS Publishing Company resources, visit our website at www.csspub.com or email us at custserv@csspub.com or call (800) 241-4056.

ISBN-10: 0-7880-2439-6   PRINTED IN U.S.A.

To the good Presbyterians
— both black and white —
of Liberty Hill, South Carolina

The Liberty Hill Presbyterian Church as it appeared in the 1980s. From the Leininger family collection.

Table Of Contents

Foreword   7
   by Reverend Doctor Thomas W. Horton Jr.
   Executive Presbyter, Bethel Presbytery

Introduction   11

Chapter 1   15
   The Seeds Of Conflict

Chapter 2   23
   Church Reunion

Chapter 3   39
   The Pot Boils Over

Chapter 4   51
   Looking Back ... And Forward

Appendix   63
   A Divided Church   65
   The Awakening Of Rip Van Winkle   75

Endnotes   83

The successor to the Liberty Hill United Presbyterian Church is Messiah Presbyterian. The new building was constructed to replace the structure that was in such dire need of repair. From the Gaither family collection.

The exterior of the Liberty Hill United Presbyterian Church as it appeared in the early 1980s. The 2x4s strategically placed to stabilize the structure are on the other side of the building. From the Gaither family collection.

Foreword

Ironically, it was his romantic, individualistic sense which kept the Southerner from really finding God but which prevented him from ever forgetting God. He was haunted by God....

He (the Southerner) is cut off from the past but haunted by it; he cannot use it, but he cannot forget it. As for the world around him today and the ultimate meaning of the world, though he has many hints within his life which carry universal and eternal meanings, he is seldom able to read them. Here again he is touched by the dream of completeness, he is haunted by God. This is his blessing and this is his curse.[1]

This story is the story of Southern people, both black and white, haunted by God. Eager to be the "people of God," and willing to become a new creation, and still bound to the past by invisible bonds, separated by invisible boundaries, and enthralled by a life that has past, present, and future so inextricably entwined, they could not step over the barriers.

It was sad to see a whole people — and they were a whole people, though different as to race — sad to see them touch and move on. Like those cascading bubbles blown from soapsuds, each full of its own beauty and fragility, touching in the breeze, bounding away, and going on and on to the end without change.

I watched this drama, and that's what it was, while it was taking place. I watched the struggle, the hopes, the dreams, the excitement — and at the same time the agonies, the hostilities, the suspicions, the dropped hands of futilities spent and gone away. I saw a people, a Christian people, some black, some white, dance a macabre cotillion of hope, frustration, and disappointment; and at the same time, a dance of defeat and an impossible dream because it simply couldn't happen then.

I watched the young pastor who wrote this account struggle to do and say and hope the right things. But he did not do or say or hope exactly as the situation demanded. I saw blacks, young and old, suffer the eternal frustration of holding onto two worlds, needing and wanting each, and getting neither. I saw whites, caring, loving, but adamantly living in two worlds also, and the former overcame the latter, and nothing happened. Now both groups are "haunted by God."

The real tragedy is that both congregations described herein could have been involved in an experiment of excitement and hope and promise, but neither made it. Yet as they continue as they were, there is still hope and love and caring and action that says, "We are still the people of God in this place!" And they are! The tragic tale unfolds, and goes on and on.

David Leininger has written a story that is, at the same time, noble, exciting, comical, and tragic. I know David as a strong, hopeful, fearless, and courageous leader of the church. I know those members of the church — leaders, officers, members, followers, descendants of the original, and new people to the ongoing tale. I know the blacks, too, but not as well; I know their dreams, their hopes, and maybe most importantly of all, I know they want their own church how it is, where it is, and where it wants to go. The collision of these two courses, black and white, will someday have to be dealt with, but not now. I watched this drama unfold, rejoiced that it started at all, then wept that it stopped without success. Maybe the larger church should have gotten into it sooner, or harder, or with more resources, or with more leadership, but I doubt it. This was a quiet, but powerful, undulating of the spiritual and psychological seas of a people in a community that had to deal with it themselves.

Read the story. I know you will be able to see many, many places where other kinds of action are indicated, or other kinds of responses should have been made or said. There was so much naiveté, so much brashness that came to nothing, and so much foolishness. Yet, there was so much hope and so much love and so much real and raw emotion described that the heart aches and wonders what to do. From these pages a phoenix can arise, a new bird of expectancy. From the ashes of seeming defeat, a new cause can spring forth with power, but it will take a new day, a new leader, and a new realm of concepts. Until then, they will all be "haunted by God." This book can help someday when the time is right. Read it, mull it over, think about it, and pray that someday a people haunted by God will emerge as a people overwhelmed by God and a new creation of his love.

> Thomas W. Horton Jr.
> Executive Presbyter
> Bethel Presbytery
> Presbyterian Church (USA)
> Rock Hill, South Carolina

The interior of the Liberty Hill Presbyterian Church in the 1980s as seen from the "slave gallery" (balcony) where slaves were allowed to worship prior to the War between the States. The loveseat behind the pulpit was a gift to the church in the 1880s and qualified as a genuine antique. During David Leininger's tenure, he insists that "at 250 pounds or so, I took my life in my hands every time I sat down." It has since been restored and strengthened. From the Leininger family collection.

Introduction

Conflict is no fun. That no one would deny. However, conflict can be a process by which everyone involved grows and matures in ways which never would have occurred had not the conflict come into being.

This book is the story of such a conflict, the story of an attempt to bring two churches — one black, one white, both Presbyterian — into closer fellowship. I wish I could report that there is a happy ending to the struggle, but at this writing, there is not, at least in my view. Perhaps some others of those who were deeply involved might say that the conflict is indeed happily over and will surface never again. At any rate, there is obviously still some conflict left, even if no more than between the two positions.

The organization of the material is relatively chronological. It begins with a brief look at the roots of the problem of the division between the races in America. It continues with the events that precipitated a particularly painful situation in the little village of Liberty Hill, South Carolina, and what actually took place. Finally, we consider what might have been done better — what might have brought about a more satisfactory outcome. Included as an appendix are two sermons I preached as the story unfolded.

You will note that there are what seem to me to be a plethora of "I's" in this book. As a writer, my training and inclination has always been to avoid "I" as much as possible, but since this is a very personal story, there really was not much choice. To those who share that sensitivity, "I" apologize.

For the benefit of readers who are not familiar with the presbyterian system of church government, some points of clarification should probably be made concerning some of the terms to be encountered here. Within the presbyterian system there are four levels of ecclesiastical authority: on the local level, the SESSION is the group of representatives elected by the congregation to administer church activities — those representatives are called ELDERS. The session might be thought of as comparable to the

Administrative Board in the Methodist Church, the Church Council in a Lutheran Church, or the Vestry in an Episcopal Church. Just above the session, exercising authority on a regional level and composed of ministers and elders from each of the congregations within its jurisdiction, is the PRESBYTERY. Several presbyteries come together to form the SYNOD. Then the most inclusive governing body which represents all the churches, all the presbyteries, and all the synods is the GENERAL ASSEMBLY. Much more could be said about all of these terms, but for the purposes of understanding what will be encountered in this volume, that brief explanation should suffice.

Most non-Presbyterians who are interested in "churchy" things are probably aware that all Presbyterians are not members of the same denomination — there is the Presbyterian Church (USA) of which I am a part, the Associate Reformed Presbyterian Church, the Presbyterian Church in America, the Orthodox Presbyterian Church, the Bible Presbyterian Church, the Cumberland Presbyterian Church, to name several. The denomination I serve came into being in 1983 with the reunion of this nation's two largest presbyterian bodies healing a division which had existed since the Civil War. This book deals with the effect of that reunion on the two small churches in Liberty Hill.

There are a number of people who deserve thanks for their help in this project: my friend and colleague in ministry, the Reverend Clark Wiser; my friend and doctoral advisor, the Reverend Doctor Merwyn S. Johnson of Erskine Seminary; my friend and brother in Christ, William Gaither, who lived through this story with me; and my friend, mentor, and Executive Presbyter, the Reverend Doctor Thomas W. Horton Jr. Each graciously suffered through several drafts of the manuscript offering constructive criticism and helpful suggestions. Special thanks are due to Doctor Horton for his willingness to provide the Foreword to this work. Particular thanks are also due to my long-suffering and delightful wife, Christie. To each of them goes a good deal of credit for this final product. For any mistakes contained herein, the blame is entirely my own.

I hope that I have grown for having been a part of this story. I would hope that the citizens of Liberty Hill have also grown for their own participation, no matter what position they took on the issues involved.

William Gaither, Clerk of Session for the Liberty Hill United Presbyterian Church in the mid-1980s. He continues to be very active in church affairs and is currently a Commissioned Lay Pastor in Providence Presbytery, the successor to the Bethel and Fairfield-McLellan Presbyteries following the reunion of the northern and southern streams of the Presbyterian Church (USA). From the Gaither family collection.

The Leininger family during the early 1980s as the events of the story unfold: the author along with wife, Christie, and son, David. From the Leininger family collection.

Chapter 1

The Seeds of Conflict

It is hard to say just where the problem began. Perhaps one could go all the way back to the Garden of Eden and the sinfulness of humanity to explain it, and certainly that would be legitimate. Perhaps one could go back to the difficulties caused in this nation because of the institution of slavery, and that, too, would be legitimate. Perhaps one could look to the problems of reconstruction after the Civil War and find some roots for the problem — again, probably legitimate. At any rate, for whatever reason, we live in a society which tends to be divided along racial lines, despite some massive governmental efforts over more than a quarter century to obliterate those lines.

Frankly, the government has done an excellent job in overcoming the inherent difficulties of centuries of prejudice and division. The various civil rights acts of the mid-'60s and since have moved American society in giant strides toward being one in which race plays no part. But the one area where government has not been able to move is in the church — where the government is concerned, the church is sacrosanct. Because of constitutional guarantees concerning the freedom of religion, neither federal nor state nor local authorities have been able to have any effect on racism within the walls of the institutional church. The result is that the church in this nation remains almost as completely segregated as it has been since reconstruction.

Of course, almost every church decries segregation under the steeple. Official pronouncements consistently affirm that "God is no respecter of persons." The social statements of the mainline denominations continually call for the eradication of racism.

Within the history of the denomination in which I serve, the Presbyterian Church (USA), there have been weighty declarations concerning the depth of the problem. For example, this from a study paper prepared by our General Assembly Mission Board called

"Partnership Toward a Culturally Plural Church" which was adopted by our General Assembly in 1979:

> *While progress has been made, eradication of racism continues to be an unfinished item, always standing in the way of our Church becoming a culturally plural church, where people of all races, cultures, and backgrounds can all join hands as sisters and brothers in Christ and realize the wholeness and unity of the church. Racism in the Presbyterian Church in the United States exists and continues whenever inequality based on racial differences is observed, presumed, or felt. Racism has prevented racial ethnic groups from full and equitable participation ... it has afflicted and impoverished the hearts and perspectives of the white majority; it has impeded the mission of the church; and it has contributed to profound social and economic injustices.*[2]

Our confessional position affirms the same attitude. For example, this from The Confession of 1967:

> *God has created the peoples of the earth to be one universal family. In His reconciling love He overcomes the barriers between brothers and breaks down every form of discrimination based on racial or ethnic difference, real or imaginary. The church is called to bring all men to receive and uphold one another as persons in all relationships of life: in employment, housing, education, leisure, marriage, family, church, and the exercise of political rights. Therefore the church labors for the abolition of all racial discrimination and ministers to those injured by it. Congregations, individuals, or groups of Christians who exclude, dominate, or patronize their fellowmen, however subtly, resist the Spirit of God and bring contempt on the faith which they profess.*[3]

Both are excellent statements and most assuredly reflect the witness of scripture. The goal is a color-blind church. But, unfortunately, neither these nor the similar words found in other Christian traditions have appeared to have much effect — certainly not much within the local congregations.

That is sad. Of all the institutions in society which should lead the way in breaking down the barriers between people of different races, one would think that the organization that leads the way in breaking down the barriers between people and God would be the one to do the job. "Reconciliation" is a watchword, but precious little reconciliation has taken place between blacks and whites in American churches. Sad.

With that kind of milieu I suppose it should not be surprising that what occurred in the little village of Liberty Hill, South Carolina, in 1983-84 should have caused such a furor. Two congregations — one black, one white — attempted to breach that racial barrier in a most tentative manner with the result that not a few ended up disillusioned, disheartened, and distressed.

Located approximately an hour north of Columbia and twenty minutes northwest of Camden, Liberty Hill is very much "Old South." There are large antebellum homes interspersed here and there with unpainted shacks. No one need have any difficulty in imagining which are occupied by whom. There is little fraternization between blacks and whites except on a level that respects the other's "position."

The village at one time was a thriving community. Prior to the Civil War, there were active plantations all around producing any number of agricultural products. There were several stores in the town, a doctor's office, a library, even a school, which at times educated as many as seventy students. Families were large and prosperous. With the advent of hostilities between the states, Liberty Hill fell victim to the ravages of the conflict, even to the extent of playing unwilling hostess to the armies of General Sherman for ten days on his march through the South. The area was made desolate and never recovered again.

Despite all that, there have been moments of glory for Liberty Hill in intervening years. Several prominent citizens have called the village their home. The most well known among them was even elected governor of South Carolina, John G. Richards Jr., who served from 1927 to 1931. Some of Governor Richards' children remained prominent members of the community.

These days there is little activity in the village — at the time of these events, there was a post office that the government regularly tried to close because of lack of business, a general store which *was* closed for lack of business, a community center that was built in the '30s with WPA money that most of the time stood idle, and two churches. Some farming went on, but not much — most of the population (approximately 100 at the last census) is retired. Those not retired generally traveled to Camden, Columbia, or Lancaster to work.

The two churches are the real center of community life. The white congregation was founded in 1851 during the halcyon days of the town; the black congregation was founded in 1873 during the depths of the reconstruction. Both churches are presbyterian in government but have been affiliated with different presbyterian bodies for much of their history. What precipitated the crisis in Liberty Hill was the merger in 1983 of those two denominations.

By way of background, Presbyterians in America were essentially a united body until the Civil War. However, the General Assembly of 1861 adopted certain resolutions to which the southern delegates could not agree without making themselves traitors to their own new nation, the Confederate States of America. The result was a forced split of Presbyterians on this continent — the Presbyterian Church in the United States of America and the Presbyterian Church in the Confederate States of America. One might think that with the end of the war there would have been a reunion of these two presbyterian bodies, but such was not the case. The church in the North eventually came to be known as the United Presbyterian Church in the United States of America (UPCUSA); the church in the South would be known as the Presbyterian Church in the United States (PCUS). To be sure, there were attempts through the years to effect such a reunion but to no avail, at least not until 1983.

Needless to say, the little congregation in Liberty Hill became a part of the Confederate church. The minister (the father of Governor Richards, by the way) even resigned to enlist as a chaplain for the confederate troops. He returned after the war and eventually served that church for 28 years, the longest pastorate in the congregation's history.

By the time the war was over, massive changes had taken place in the community. Not only had the economy been destroyed but now the blacks in town were full-fledged American citizens. Blacks and whites had worshiped together prior to the fighting (the blacks in their own "slave gallery" of course) and continued to do so for a time. But eventually, as a reflection of what was going on with reconstruction, the black worshipers petitioned the presbytery for the formation of their own congregation — the Liberty Hill Colored Presbyterian Church. The request was granted in 1873.

Land for the black congregation was donated some 300 yards from the white church, a building was constructed and services were begun there. The two village congregations continued as members of the same denomination for some years until the black worshipers responded to what was euphemistically called "the colored work" of the presbyterians in the North, an effort on the part of churches above the Mason-Dixon line to offer aid and encouragement to poor, black congregations in the South. One of the results of that work was that the Liberty Hill Colored Presbyterian Church became officially affiliated with their northern brothers and sisters. Despite their proximity, the white and black churches in the village lost virtually all contact ... and they were happy that way.

Neither church had any numerical or financial strength. By 1981, when I was called as a seminary student to serve the white congregation, there were only about a dozen people who regularly came to services. The black congregation was not much different. The white church met every Sunday at 11 a.m. as they had done for years and years; the black church had been reduced to meeting every other Sunday, sharing a part-time pastor with another small black congregation some forty miles away. Both churches were receiving financial support from their denominations.

The presbytery of which the white church was a part had considered recommending the closing of the facility but was convinced by some of the members that a real ministry could be centered in that congregation which sought to meet the needs of vacationers to Lake Wateree some nine miles away. In 1977, a weekly outdoor worship service had been established to run from the first Sunday in June through Labor Day, and by 1980, there were about forty people who would attend from week to week. Presbytery decided that this was indeed a valid ministry so the congregation was not encouraged to disband.

I really hate to admit it, but for the first two years I spent serving the white congregation, I had no idea about the situation in the black church. I had no knowledge of the people; I did not know the minister; I did not even know that their worship schedule was different from ours. Worst of all, I made no attempt to know any of that. I look back on it now and try to make excuses for my ignorance and disinterest (too busy with school, and the like), but none are really valid.

As to my own position concerning racial matters, I would have to call myself benevolently neutral, if such an animal could exist. I realize that where injustice is concerned, neutrality is not a viable option for a Christian. To be sure, there is nothing very benevolent about acquiescing to the unfair treatment of any human being. Suffice it to say that I appreciated the efforts that blacks had made to reach equality in American society, but they had done so without the benefit of any activism on my part. In looking back on it now, I can only say *"Mea culpa; mea culpa."*

One could be generous and say that my benevolent neutrality was shared by many of the other folks in my congregation — there were some. But I fear that even such a statement would be a bit too generous. In more cases than I would care to note, there was evidence of a genuinely active prejudice against blacks.

As I said earlier, Liberty Hill is very much "Old South" and racial attitudes tend to reflect that. Soon after I became a part of the community, I had occasion to visit with a dear ninety-year-old lady who was the matriarch of one of the village's leading families. During the course of our wide-ranging conversation, we began discussing what it had been like to be the mistress of her large antebellum home since almost the beginning of the twentieth century. She confessed that there had been some difficulties in managing it all, then she mentioned that she thought that the greatest tragedy to ever befall our nation was the freeing of the slaves — it left no one to do any work. I started to laugh, thinking that she was having fun with the young preacher, but fortunately, I held back. She was entirely serious. I was more than a little taken aback. After all, that was the 1980s — *no one* thought like that any more, or so I thought. I had been brought up and lived all my life up to this point in what I now realize was a relatively enlightened, cosmopolitan atmosphere. I had been taught that racial attitudes like hers were a relic of a benighted past. I was obviously wrong.

But so saying, it should be pointed out that there were indeed a number of progressive thinking people in the community who would have recoiled as I did at hearing such racist statements. It is to these folks that credit should be given for the attempts to bring black and white worshipers in Liberty Hill together again after a separation of more than 100 years. They, as well as I, had been caught in the middle of a racial situation which was not to our liking, but with which we had been able to come to terms.

The interior of the Liberty Hill United Presbyterian Church. It was in this sanctuary that the joint Christmas program was held in December 1983. From the Leininger family collection.

The Fellowship Hall of the Liberty Hill Presbyterian Church where members of both the black and white congregations gathered following the Christmas program in December 1983. From the Leininger family collection.

Chapter 2
Church Reunion

As noted, what precipitated the events that occurred in that quiet little community was the reunion of the two largest presbyterian denominations in the country. After years of negotiation, The UPCUSA and the PCUS voted to become one body: The Presbyterian Church (USA). The historic day was June 10, 1983.

There had been wide support for such a reunion in many parts of the nation, but in much of the South (at least among many PCUS churches), there was only lukewarm enthusiasm for it at best. The division which had seen its beginning with the Civil War had continued for more than 120 years, persisting because the northern and southern branches of presbyterianism assumed different ecclesiastical positions concerning the understanding of connectional relationships. In simple terms, the UPCUSA took the view that the higher governing bodies of the church were called to exercise regulatory authority over those bodies under their control; the PCUS took the view that the higher governing bodies were called to facilitate the ministries of those bodies under their control. Needless to say, such a statement is an oversimplification, but the difference in emphasis was real.

Another reason for some of the southern reluctance was that there was a considerable geographical overlap between the two denominations concerning congregations affiliated with each. Churches of the former PCUS could be found in seventeen states, while churches of the UPCUSA were in all fifty. A major realignment would be necessary — presbytery and synod boundaries would have to be redrawn. Some of the smaller black congregations in the South (which were almost all affiliated with the Northern church) were concerned about being "swallowed up" and losing any clout they had in their local areas. In the realignment process, they could see a danger of being overwhelmed by the larger and more prosperous white congregations. After all, it would be with those same powerful, white congregations that the black churches would become members of the new presbyteries to be established after reunion.

A further reason for reluctance on the part of PCUS churches was a similar fear of being "swallowed up," but on the national level. After all, the UPCUSA had two-and-a-half times as many members as the PCUS and the Southerners could envision being outvoted in General Assembly on any issue of particular concern.

Sadly, part of the opposition within southern churches came as a result of some of the most blatant lies that I had ever heard. People were being told that if reunion passed they would no longer be able to call their own pastors — churches would have to take whatever ministers the denomination would send them. Folks were hearing that the new denomination would come in and take ownership of buildings and cemeteries. They were hearing that the "Yankees" were nothing more than a bunch of heretics who did not believe in the Bible or historic Christian doctrine. Some of the stories were incredible. They were nothing but lies, but that made no difference. No matter who would try to correct the information, for far too many life-long Presbyterians, the reunion waters had been irretrievably poisoned.

I personally opposed the reunion, not because of the stupid stories, but for other reasons. I was convinced that the agreements which had been negotiated failed to address some very important issues concerning theological positions, administrative problems, and disciplinary questions. Had I had the opportunity to vote on the question (which I did not as a seminary student), I would have voted against it. However, I further took the position that I would accept the outcome of the vote as God's will for the church and would work to support whatever might eventuate. I shared my position with the congregation and heard that my basic feelings were shared by many. (I have since reversed my opinion and have become a wholehearted supporter of reunion.)

One of the concerns that was also held in Liberty Hill dealt with the situation existing with the two little churches. As mentioned, neither congregation was exceptionally strong either financially or numerically (although the PCUS church was by this time self-supporting), and there was concern that, with reunion, the congregations would be forced to join as one in the new denomination. There were assurances all around that such would not be the case, but the worries persisted nonetheless.

Thus, the negotiating process to effect reunion was long and arduous but finally won the support of the vast majority of American Presbyterians. The vote came and went on June 10, and to no one's surprise, reunion was a reality — the UPCUSA and the PCUS were now the PCUSA. That meant that the two little Liberty Hill churches, separated by a graveyard, a stand of trees, and a racial/cultural gulf greater than the one between Lazarus and Dives were now members of the same denomination.

It would be lovely to say that once the national church became reunited, the little churches in Liberty Hill saw the wisdom of such an action at their own level and decided to do the same. After all, the two churches were originally one until the difficulties of reconstruction. It would not be a merger; it would legitimately be a reunion. That is nothing more than wishful thinking. What actually occurred was both encouraging and discouraging at the same time.

The encouraging thing was the position taken by the session of the former PCUS congregation in its regular meeting on June 12, two days after the action taken by the General Assemblies in Atlanta. Near the end of that Sunday afternoon meeting, one of the elders said that since the two churches in the village were now members of the same denomination, we should make some efforts at getting to know our PCUSA neighbors with an eye to building some fraternal relationships. The rest of the session unanimously agreed.

I recall feeling that I would like to have kissed the man for his suggestion. I had felt the same way he did about doing some fence-mending (or tearing-down, as the case happened to be), but was a bit concerned about being the one to raise the possibility. After all, I was the new boy on the block and, despite having been these folks' minister for the past two years, I was afraid I was still perceived as something of an outsider. I was glad that the resolution was introduced and adopted.

Since we had had absolutely no contact with the other congregation up to this point, the plan of action was for one of the elders to find out the names of the officers of the black church (including the minister) and then report back to the session with the information. Once that was accomplished, I was commissioned to contact my counterpart in the neighboring pulpit (the Reverend Jesse L. Moore, as I was to learn) to simply get acquainted and begin to feel out possibilities for some joint efforts.

In the meantime, new information came to light that, in my mind, made our mission of fence-mending all the more urgent — it was learned that the black congregation wanted to build a new church. Under normal circumstances, that would have been no problem. Generally, when a local church feels the need and the ability to handle such a thing, it is a time for celebration. However, in this particular instance, the Liberty Hill United Presbyterian Church (the LHUPC, as the black congregation was known — the white church was known as the Liberty Hill Presbyterian Church, the LHPC) was not considering building to accommodate an increase in membership. The number on roll was only about forty members with only half of them in attendance at their semi-monthly services. They were simply looking to replace their current structure which was quite literally falling down around their ears. The building in which they were worshiping was only upright because it was braced that way by a series of strategically placed 2x4s. Without those braces, the building would have been a pile of rubble. In other circumstances, one could have hardly objected to that congregation's desire for a new facility. But now that there was another church building of the same denomination as theirs only 300 yards away (a building which was in excellent condition, by the way), it made no sense to me to see thousands of dollars spent to preserve a division which had no more need of existence.

By this time, I was getting excited about the possibilities despite the fact that I had never taken much of a leadership role in racial matters in the past. I had known that there would be certain difficulties concerning reunion because of the racial situation in the South, but I began to see that the Lord was giving an opportunity to the Christians in this sleepy little village to provide a witness, not only to the new church but to the whole world, of what could be done when the gospel was taken seriously. Not only were the black and white Presbyterians in Liberty Hill now members of the same denomination, but a day could soon come when they might be members of the same congregation — an incredible event in the rural South.

One of the members of my congregation who was a contractor was approached to consult with the LHUPC session and offer a bid on the building they envisioned. I told him that he might mention to them the possibility of simply using the LHPC facilities rather than spending the money necessary to erect a new structure. A few days after that meeting, the contractor reported to me that he had passed on my proposal, but it was met with a resoundingly negative response. Additionally, he told me that the building that was being discussed would cost far more money than the approximately $25,000 the congregation had saved to pay for it with the result that all their plans were going to have to be scaled down to a considerable degree.

Looking back on it now, I realize that if the situation had been reversed, had it been *my* church building that someone was asking me to abandon, I probably would have reacted just as negatively. After all, holy ground is no less holy just because the building on it is in disrepair. Nonetheless, I was distressed at the time by the reaction of the black congregation. I could not believe that they could not see God's hand in all this moving us toward one racially inclusive church. Ah well, we preacher types are often frustrated when people miss what we consider our divinely inspired insight.

Meanwhile, Jesse Moore and I made efforts at getting together to follow up on becoming acquainted. Somehow, we just could not seem to manage — we were simply never able to get our schedules to mesh. He lived almost an hour away from Liberty Hill and was unable to travel at will — I was to learn later that Jesse was totally blind, the result of an advanced diabetic condition. As it turned out, it would take more than two months after that June 12 session meeting for the pastors to meet face-to-face.

In the interim, other problems were beginning to take my attention. The June reunion had prompted a number of nearby presbyterian congregations to totally withdraw from the new denomination and far too many of them because of the lies that had been told. Sadly, there were folks in those churches who disagreed with the decisions to withdraw and felt themselves ostracized and abandoned by people whom they had considered dear Christian friends for years. Some who felt that way began to come to our summer lakeside services that, by this time, had grown to an average attendance of about 175 per week. These folks began to seek me out concerning their difficulties. I had no answers for them other than to suggest that they put away bitterness and seek affiliation with congregations in which they could be comfortable. I was hoping that some of them would find their way to the Liberty Hill church but such was not to be.

Concerning what had been happening with the two little congregations, I was also beginning to get some static. Support for making any joint efforts, no matter what form they might take, was apparently not as widespread as I might have hoped. In fact, I was hearing from some folks that they would not stand for having any kind of real relationship between the two congregations, much less agree to any reunion of the two. They made it very plain that if such a reunion should ever occur, they would find themselves another church.

Vacation time came. My family and I had planned for some months to attend the annual Bible Conference which is held at Massanetta Springs, Virginia, an event that has been held for many years and consistently attracts as speakers some of the best preachers in America. This was the first time I had been back to Massanetta in many years. As a boy growing up in a presbyterian manse, we had come to Massanetta for a number of those summer conferences and my memories of them were always terrific. As a teenager, I fell in love at Massanetta any number of times — after all, where one finds preachers' families, one finds preachers' daughters. (Isn't God good?) Now that I was grown, my interests were more theological than biological but I was looking forward to it nonetheless.

One evening I heard George Docherty, the former minister of New York Avenue Presbyterian Church in Washington, DC, recall describing the vacation at Massanetta to his mother. He told her that the day began with a time of personal devotions out on the grassy slopes of the Shenandoah Valley. It would continue with breakfast, then a worship service at 9:00, a Bible study at 10:00, then a panel discussion of some sort on a religious subject at 11:00, followed by lunch. In the afternoon, there would be workshops dealing with improving professional skills followed by some free time and then supper. The evening would offer a worship service at 7:00 followed by another service at 8:00 with the night finally coming to a close after a time of quiet reflection under a star-filled sky. Doctor Docherty reported that his mother's reaction was, "That's a *vacation*?" To him it was, and to me and my family it was. We all looked forward to it.

Since the reunion decision had only passed some seven weeks before, it was still a topic of considerable conversation wherever any Presbyterians gathered and Massanetta was no exception. One of those morning panel discussions had been set aside to consider the topic of our now reunited church and I was interested in hearing the discussion. There was a good deal of back-slapping, conviviality, and congratulations among the panel members. After all, these men had all been very much in favor of the move and now their side had carried the day, and overwhelmingly at that. One man even laughingly said something to the effect that "I'd bet that some of those poor southern delegates who had opposed reunion all along but who came to Atlanta and voted for it anyway because the Spirit of God *made* them do it ended up asking themselves on the way home, 'What did I do?' Ha, ha, ha!"

I was incensed. Obviously, none of these fellows had ever had anyone come to them in tears because they had been thrown out of their church. Obviously, none of these fellows had ever been told by some pretty faithful members that they would leave the church if any interracial activities with blacks were considered. Obviously, none of these fellows were in presbyteries where churches were leaving the new denomination lock, stock, and barrel. It seemed to me that all reunion meant to these people, who were already big fish in the presbyterian pond, was that they would now be big fish in an even bigger pond. The only personal impact of reunion on them would be that sooner or later they would have to memorize a new address for denominational headquarters. As I say, I was incensed ... and I told them so.

As I stood at the microphone on the floor of that open-air conference hall, I recounted some of the stories of what had been happening in my part of the country since reunion. Now, all the laughter and joking stopped. These were stories with which these panel members were not familiar at all. Up to this point, I doubt that any of them had had any idea of what might really happen in the South once reunion became a reality. Now they knew.

One asked, "What can we do to help you?"

I responded, "Pray. Pray like crazy."

Once vacation was over, we returned to Liberty Hill in the hope that a meeting between Jesse Moore and myself could finally be arranged. He had previously indicated that he would be pleased to get together with me and discuss our session's thinking. Finally, one Sunday afternoon near the end of August, we met one another face-to-face for the first time.

He telephoned me just before he was to arrive and asked if I would mind his bringing along one of the lay leaders of his congregation, a Mr. William Gaither, the LHUPC Clerk of Session, the most prestigious non-professional position in a local presbyterian church. I had no objection, so they both came over. We sat and talked in my living room for almost an hour and a half that day, and I confess that I was totally non-plussed by what I heard.

The first thing that caught me by surprise was the feeling expressed by both men that they were none too thrilled with the fact that the UPCUSA and the PCUS had reunited. It had been my understanding that the vote in their presbytery had been unanimously in favor of the move, and apparently these men had indeed voted for the action but were now not all that pleased about it. Both of them even went so far as to say that should there be any move whatsoever on the part of the new denomination to force our two congregations to reunite, they would leave the PCUSA altogether. I tried to put their minds at ease on that point, as I had tried to do for the white congregation, a process I felt should have been unnecessary for two men who should have known better than to be concerned.

Needless to say, they were aware of my position concerning the proposed new building for their congregation. They were less than thrilled about that, also. I tried to explain to them that, under the circumstances, it seemed to be questionable stewardship to sink such significant resources into the preservation of a status quo which was no longer "quo." I further explained that I thought that we could make an incredible witness to the world of the reconciling power of the gospel if we would make such a physically visible move toward reunification. They appeared unmoved.

Mr. Moore made it clear to me that I simply did not understand. Regardless of how fine a building might be available for their use right nearby, it would not be *their* building. They had no desire to abandon property which had belonged to that congregation for years and years. After all, their parents and grandparents were buried there. This land was special.

I confess that I honestly had not thought of the problem in that light before. The dimensions of the issue were obviously greater than I had previously realized. As I sat there listening to this eloquent servant of God, I was convinced that there had to be some way to accommodate his concerns short of spending thousands of dollars to construct a new building that a small congregation could not afford. Perhaps there was a way to maintain the graveyard in its present location while constructing a walkway from there to the other sanctuary. At any rate, alternatives were not really explored. After all, we were meeting for the first time.

A further objection was raised by the clerk when he expressed concern over the future of his pastor in any move toward a reunion of the two congregations. He said, "We don't want the same thing to happen in our church as happened in our schools. When they integrated the schools, all the white principals ended up as principals and all the black principals ended up running the school bus routes." It was a valid concern and one for which I had no immediate answer.

As the conversation went on, Jesse raised an issue that took me by surprise. He said that a potential problem was what to do about interracial dating once these two congregations began to work together. He said that nature would no doubt take its course and black boys and girls and white boys and girls would begin to fraternize, one thing would lead to another, and well....

What? I could not believe my ears. Here was the old redneck stereotype — the only thing black men are interested in is white women — just couched in a new form. In my congregation there were only three teenagers. In his congregation I was sure there were not many more. None of those young people, either black or white, were limited in their social contacts to the people they would meet at church. Considering the social situation in the rural South, it seemed to me a totally unreal assumption, not to mention an incredible jump to a rather far-fetched conclusion. I was taken off guard to such an extent that I really had no reply other than, "Well, I guess we'll just have to cross that bridge when we come to it."

Both men expressed concern over my safety, something that had not even crossed my mind. Mr. Moore said, "You know they'll come after you, don't you?"

"They?" I replied. "What do you mean?"

"The Klan. The Ku Klux Klan. They won't come after me because I'm just a poor ol' blind preacher. But you're young. You have a family. Have you thought about them?"

I honestly had to say that I had not. I knew that the Ku Klux Klan was still alive and well in our part of the South, but it had not occurred to me that two tiny congregations in an obscure little village wanting to worship together would attract their attention. I finally said to my guests, "Gentlemen, I am not a masochist. I am not into pain, either for myself or for my family, but I have to say that if I am ever called upon to die for a cause, I cannot think of a cause better than this one." I really meant that then, and I mean that even today. Fortunately, I was never called upon to back up my bravado.

By the time our conversation ended, a good working relationship had been established between the three of us despite all the problems that had been surfaced. Perhaps the reason that the relationship was established at all was our candor with one another. On a practical plane, we had decided to encourage the sessions of the two churches to meet together without the ministers to explore avenues of common interest. I confess that I would have preferred to be a part of any meetings between the two bodies, but because of Jesse Moore's problems concerning travel I agreed. We closed our gathering with prayer for both guidance and fortitude as we faced the opportunities with which we had been presented.

Obviously, one cannot do justice to an hour-and-a-half conversation in just a few short paragraphs. Despite the problems that were openly discussed, and even despite the hostility that seemed to me to be seething just below the surface (espccially on the part of the clerk), there was an air of cordiality to our meeting which encouraged me as we looked to the future.

However, beyond that encouragement, I became aware that day as I had not been before of the problems that would have to be overcome if these two little churches would ever finally officially come together. There was a lot that would have to be done.

Within a few weeks, I officially reported the results of that Sunday afternoon meeting to the LHPC session including the suggestion that the two local governing bodies meet. Additionally, it was proposed that the two congregations make efforts at preparing a joint Christmas program (to which the black church agreed) with one of our elders appointed to follow up on the planning. No one indicated at the time any reservations concerning pursuit of the matter, but such reservations soon became evident from both sides.

The session of the LHUPC simply could never make arrangements to meet with our group. Our elder in charge of helping to plan the holiday program continually found himself too busy to make any arrangements. Word began to filter in from members of both congregations that doing anything cross-racially was not a particularly good idea. I was beginning to get very frustrated at the lack of progress.

As the weeks wore on and Thanksgiving approached, nothing had been accomplished at all toward our announced plan for some sort of joint Christmas service. Those members of the black congregation who were in charge of arrangements were forced to go ahead on their own without any input from us in the white church. A final planning session was scheduled with the wife of the elder who had been originally commissioned as our representative set to substitute for him, but on the day before the meeting, she came to me and said that she would be "unable" (read that "unwilling") to participate. I was distressed at the turn of events, but some hasty arrangements were made and plans were formulated for a special program to be held at 5:00 p.m. on Sunday, December 18. Individuals from both congregations would participate in a time of scripture reading and singing that would be conducted in the dilapidated LHUPC sanctuary. That would be followed by a time of light refreshment and fellowship in the educational building of the LHPC (the black congregation had neither a fellowship hall nor an educational facility).

Final plans were announced to both congregations with as much advance notice as possible. We were hoping for a good turnout, but with the reluctance that had begun to surface, we had no idea what to expect. There was no official publicity beyond the village, but word soon got around that blacks and whites were going to have a service together. Within days, the hate calls started. There were not really that many of them, but the several that came got their message across. They called to find out if what they had heard about an interracial worship was true. When informed that they had heard accurately, they let me know in no uncertain terms just what they thought of the idea, and while they were about it, what they thought about me. Some Presbyterians called to find out if the new denomination was forcing these two congregations to do this. When told that the PCUSA had nothing to do with it, they blithely ignored what they had just been told and began to berate the denomination that would force their social agenda on poor unsuspecting little communities. There was a certain amount of name-calling, but, thank God, nothing more than that.

Probably what distressed me most was the attitude of some of the members of my own congregation. There were a few that I might have anticipated would be opposed to any joint efforts between blacks and whites and who had made their feelings known several months before. Frankly, some of them pleasantly surprised me by their support for what was being done. But there were others — people whom I would have thought would be in the forefront of something like this because of their understanding of the gospel and because of their position in life — who became bitter in their opposition. To this day, I cannot fathom their reaction. I obviously had either misread them all along or had failed to surface their apparently deeply held objections. If indeed these folks had good, legitimate reasons to oppose the plan, they made no real effort to explain them to me despite repeated invitations. One can only do so much — I refuse to accept responsibility for their reticence. But I was still distressed.

The big day finally came and my wife and I got in our car for the quick ride from the one church to the other. As we arrived, I recall being delightfully surprised at the number of cars parked there. The crowd turned out to be much larger than I would have hoped — about 35 whites and 25 blacks. There were even some there who had been very vocal in their displeasure with the whole concept. All in all, nearly everyone in attendance was soon enraptured by the proceedings. The music was exciting and the scriptures inspiring. The presence of the Holy Spirit was almost palpable. It was an incredible experience. It seemed as if a miracle had taken place. Both during the service and in the car on the way back to the fellowship hall of our church, my wife was in tears because she had been so moved by what had taken place.

Within a few minutes, both black and white worshipers were gathered for the refreshments and something else incredible happened — they actually sat down and ate together, something that was just not done in that culture. There had been other times when I had seen blacks and whites in Liberty Hill around food — there had been special dinners where some of the black maids had been asked to help with the serving and so on. I had been surprised on such occasions that the white folks would sit down to the table, enjoy the meal and each other, all the while ignoring the black folks who were simply standing around after having helped to handle some of the work. In my naiveté, I had invited the black folks to sit down and join us, but I soon learned that this sort of thing just did not happen in the rural South.

Some years ago the late Harry Golden, the editor of the *Carolina Israelite*, facetiously made a proposal during the days when the nation was wracked with dissension over the integration of the schools. He suggested that we take out all the desks — just have the students stand as they worked. His contention was that white folks did not seem to mind *standing* with black folks; they would just not *sit* together. Take out the school desks; solve the problem. No one ever took him up on that, but it was an interesting thought at the time.

But now, on this special evening, no one had to worry about taking anything out. This was not school but church. If anything, in our culture it was a place where even more passionate concern could be aroused. Still, black and white were not only sitting together but eating together. Incredible.

The conversation was free and easy. Everyone appeared to enjoy the evening immensely. I know I did.

There were a few strains, but nothing major. One that comes to mind is the extra effort that one of our dear white ladies expended in making small talk. She would come up to one black after another, make their acquaintance, learn their names, and then in the friendliest, most jovial manner one could imagine, let them know who in the white community probably *owned* their grandfather. I felt like strangling her.

Despite the occasional glitch like that, the evening was spectacular — so spectacular, in fact, that the black congregation was invited to join with the white congregation the following Sunday morning for 11:00 a.m. worship. After all, the following Sunday would be Christmas Day, and since their own minister was scheduled to conduct services in his alternate congregation, the black citizens of Liberty Hill would not have the opportunity to worship unless they traveled to another town. The one request made was that the LHUPC choir provide some special music for the service which they readily agreed to do.

Christmas Eve intervened between the two joint services. My congregation was used to having a candlelight Christmas Eve service each year and 1983 would be no exception. For the first time, several black faces were in the congregation and without any special invitation. One of those was the LHUPC Clerk of Session, a man who had done a 180-degree turn in his attitude toward interracial cooperation since that first meeting back in August. That night, I probably glowed like the candles in the windows.

The worship the next day was as marvelous as I could have hoped. The congregation was fairly evenly divided between black and white. An almost entirely musical service was conducted with special selections from the black choir, from my wife and I (who constituted the nearest thing to a choir that the white congregation had), and that same William Gaither who possessed a fine tenor voice. Again, the response of the congregation seemed most positive and encouraged me to plan the next step — a joint communion service on the first Sunday in February, Race Relations Sunday, six weeks hence, a move which had already been approved by our session.

Christmas afternoon, my pregnant wife, our three-year-old son, and I took off from Liberty Hill for a ten-day vacation, the traditional visit to our families at the holiday. Arrangements had previously been made to fill my pulpit for the following Sunday, but nothing had been done about providing special music for the worship, a task which either my bride or myself normally fulfilled. Under the circumstances, and with things going as well as they were in the relationship between the two congregations, I asked William Gaither if he might be willing to sing at our 11:00 a.m. worship on January 1 before he had to go to his own church for their service which was scheduled for noon. He graciously agreed, so preparations were now complete.

I wish I could put my finger on what caused the change in the relationship between William Gaither and me. To be honest, the hostility that I sensed in him back in August (which he will deny to this day, by the way) had made me very uneasy. I had heard before I ever met the man that he could be difficult and unbending. In fact, he had aroused more than a little ire among the white citizens of

Liberty Hill some years before by instituting a suit against the local school system in nearby Camden (where Liberty Hill children went), which forced an end to some districting practices that allowed for *de facto* segregation. My initial impression of him tended to validate what I had heard, but over the course of several months of telephone calls back and forth and informal meetings to plan proposed activities, I found a different man entirely. I am certain that the assessment of William as difficult was and is perfectly valid if what qualifies a man as difficult is that he will not be walked over. But unbending? Not at all. He had done everything in his power to get our joint worship efforts to go smoothly despite the reservations he obviously had just a few months before — a fairly major "bend" in my view. At any rate, this new friendship was one of the nicest Christmas presents I received that year.

As my family and I drove away from Liberty Hill, we thought we were leaving a tranquil, happy little town, content in its celebration of a newly experienced oneness in the Savior whose birth we were all celebrating. How wrong we were.

Chapter 3
The Pot Boils Over

During the week and a half that I was gone, the opposition that had been fairly silent during the recent joint ventures between the two churches suddenly found its voice. Perhaps they just needed me to be away before they could make their feelings known. At any rate, they began letting one another know what a disastrous thing all this interracial nonsense was, letting the members of the LHPC session know of their displeasure, and finally, upon my return, letting me know that they were counting on the fact that I would soon cease and desist from all my troublemaking.

I confess I was more than a little taken aback by it all. It had seemed to me that things had been going swimmingly. A number of people in both congregations had expressed sincere pleasure over the joint services we had had. Plans had already been announced for the historic communion service that was coming up and no one had expressed reservations. Things had been going well. Too well, perhaps.

My wife even commented to me once the opposition began to make itself known, "You know, David, things have been going along just too smoothly. The real miracle here is that the problems haven't surfaced until now." She was right. Once we had finally gotten things off the ground last August, there really had been only the most minor of difficulties. After all, what we were doing was flying in the face of centuries of rural southern tradition. When it comes right down to it, we were probably very lucky that the potential violence of which Jesse Moore had warned had never occurred.

Opposition made no difference to me in this case, though. I was utterly convinced that what we had been doing was right in the eyes of a God who sent his Son to die for all of us, regardless of the color of our skin. I was equally convinced that the witness of the churches in Liberty Hill would be immeasurably enhanced by coming together in a visible demonstration of how the gospel could break the chains which bind us. I had no intention of backing off. By now, for me, the whole question had taken on the dimensions of a holy crusade.

Still the opposition came. Two ladies came to my office one afternoon to let me know that they totally disapproved of what had happened. One said that she was afraid that letting the blacks into "our" church any more would probably result in damage to our sanctuary: "You know how they live, Mr. Leininger. They live in shacks. They don't know how to take care of anything. They'll end up carving their initials in our pews." I pointed out to her that there was no evidence of any pew carving in the LHUPC sanctuary when we went in there for worship, and I had not noticed anything like that after the Christmas service we had held in "her" sanctuary. The other lady allowed as how blacks might be permitted in "our" sanctuary, but only to clean. I admit that it took every ounce of control I could muster not to throw them out of that office bodily.

After they left, I thought of that story which had gone around for so long and in so many versions about the usher in a little presbyterian church who was confronted, one Sunday morning, by the presence of an elegant and aged black man at the church door. The usher took pains to show the gentleman to a pew right down in the front of the sanctuary, came and sat down by the visitor during the worship service, and in general made sure that the man felt right at home. Later on, and after the gentleman had departed, some of the other parishioners made their objections known.

"Why did you treat that black man so well? This is a *white* church! You didn't have to make him feel all *that* welcome."

But the perspicacious usher replied, "If you noticed, that gentleman was right on up there in years. I figured that he would probably be getting to heaven before I would and that one day, *he* might even be the man at the gate. I just wanted him to remember me kindly in case I got there on the day he was the usher."

I have often wondered how some of our good church folk will react when they find out that heaven is integrated. I fear that some of them will think that they have gone to the wrong place. Come to think of it, perhaps they will have.

Later that week, during my regular pastoral visitation, I happened to call on a dear, little 89-year-old lady who had been most consistent in her support of my ministry in the community. She was one who could always be counted on to make her opinions known without any hint of dissembling. If she did not think my sermon was up to snuff, she would let me know it on the way out of church. If I had been unclear on any point, she would make it known to me in no uncertain terms. She was a delight. To me she had always been a loveable "character." Now she was upset.

As I came into her living room she said, "I'm glad you came by. I wanted to talk to you."

"Oh really? What about?" I responded.

"About *slowing down*! You're going too fast."

I knew what she was talking about, but I wanted to draw her out. "What do you mean?"

"The *race* stuff. We're just not ready for all this."

"I'm not sure I understand."

"I mean putting these two churches together. What's going to happen when you leave? Are we going to have a nigra (sic) preacher for *our* preacher? *No, sir!*"

She was genuinely stressed at this point so I tried to calm her down. "Now wait a minute. Slow down here. I'm not going anywhere, and nobody would force a preacher on you that you didn't want anyway. Tell me what you're worried about."

"These two churches have always been separate [not true] and they should always *be* separate. You're going too fast. We don't need all this interracial stuff around here."

I wanted to assuage her fears, but there was nothing I could say with the current circumstances to indicate I could give in to her wishes. Subsequent conversations indicated that she was not really opposed in principle to what was taking place. She simply let it be known that, if she had her "druthers," nothing would be done until after she was dead.

By this time, complaints about the situation were being taken outside the bounds of the community. Some folks had even gone to

Rock Hill and the office of Bethel Presbytery, the body which had authority over the white congregation in Liberty Hill, to try to get them to intervene and stop what was happening. The Executive Presbyter, Doctor Tom Horton, listened to what they had to say and told them he would look into the matter. However, he gave no hint that he would acquiesce to their demands. As a matter of fact, he was most supportive throughout the whole ordeal.

Meanwhile, the members of the LHPC session were being contacted to get them to put a stop to these joint ventures. They were informed that not only members of the white congregation, but members of the black congregation as well wanted to call a halt. Fortunately, every one of those valiant leaders let it be known that they were in perfect agreement with what had taken place so far and had no intention of censuring me on any point. But despite their vocal support, the complaints began to take their toll, and privately, one elder after another came to me to make me aware of what was going on. After all, these folks had to live together and none of them wanted to see the community divided because of something the church — the reconciler — was doing. I could not really blame them.

I contacted William Gaither, who was the *de facto* leader of the LHUPC, because of the physical distance and disability of Pastor Moore, to let him know what I had been hearing. He told me that he, too, had been hearing similar complaints from within his own fellowship. In fact, he was being accused by his people of being a co-conspirator with me to force an organic reunion of the two churches. To be sure, such was not the case and he tried to convince his congregation of that, but they remained unmollified. Regardless, Gaither remained firm in his position. We both agreed that we could not buckle under the pressure because there was a theological issue at stake here: whether or not the gospel really could make a difference in bringing people together.

Despite all the brouhaha, there were still many who indicated their backing for what had happened and any future efforts which might be considered. Not only Doctor Horton, but other ministers in the presbytery as well, indicated their enthusiasm for the progress that had been made. Individual members of my congregation also let it be known that they appreciated what had been done.

Up to this point I had never dealt with the affair from the pulpit other than making announcements concerning scheduled events. I had made no secret of my position in the matter of joint activity and even concerning what I hoped would be the eventual reunion of the two little churches. Anyone who had been interested had heard my thinking in detail, perhaps even more than they wanted. Now I was hearing that I should deal with the situation in a sermon to more fully explain the theological rationale for the efforts that had been made as well as a more complete explanation of what I saw the future to hold. It was good advice, so such a sermon was written and preached on January 22. (See Appendix.)

I wish I could say that the storm was calmed after that, but it was not. There were still some who objected to the communion service which had been authorized by the sessions and was scheduled for two weeks hence. There were still some who, despite what I thought was an exceedingly clear emphasis, could not be convinced that no reunion of the congregations would ever take place until they *both* wanted it. For some, no explanation at all would have sufficed.

As the time drew near for the Race Relations Sunday service, word came that Pastor Moore had been hospitalized. His health had been tenuous for some time and now it had finally deteriorated to the extent that it was unmanageable at home. Both of us had planned to participate in the worship with me leading the liturgy and delivering the sermon and him celebrating the sacrament of the Lord's Supper. His absence would pose a problem because, as an unordained seminary student, I was not permitted to officiate for communion. The problem was easily overcome though — another minister in Bethel Presbytery, the Reverend Richard Massey, who served as the Director of the Columbia Area Mental Health Service, volunteered to fill in.

Sunday, February 5, proved to be a historic day. There in that sleepy little Southern village, black and white came together to the table of our Lord and Savior. Blacks and whites had communed at the same table during the years of slavery and after, but never at the same time — whites were served first, then the "colored." But on this day, there was no distinction. For this one hour at least, both races came as one to their color-blind Lord. White fingers took the communion bread from trays held by black hands; black fingers lifted the cups from trays offered by white hands. Just as at Christmas, the presence of the Holy Spirit was almost palpable.

Attendance at the service was good — about 35 whites and 25 blacks. Even some of those who had been loudest in their protests were there. Only one lady made any show of her displeasure — when the communion plates were passed, she took the elements and, with great flourish, put them down untouched. I thought at the time, "It's a good thing she didn't partake — it probably would have poisoned her."

That afternoon saw the regular winter meeting of Bethel Presbytery, one to which, as a student, I was not required to go. However, it had always been my practice to attend such meetings anyway so as to better keep my congregation informed of activities on that level. Because William Gaither was active in the presbytery which oversaw the LHUPC (Fairfield-McLelland Presbytery), I invited him to attend our meeting as a guest. He was pleased to do so, and it was a pleasure to introduce him to that body that afternoon and share with them what had occurred in our village earlier that day.

One might wish that such an experience of God's grace might have served to quell any dissension, but it did not. The protests continued unabated. There were more calls to the presbytery, more complaints to the session, more harsh words to me. There were complaints about the way the interracial activities had been reported in our LHPC newsletter, even complaints about the fact that I had invited Mr. Gaither to our presbytery meeting.

Some wanted to call a congregational meeting to discuss what was going on, but doing so would have been illegal in the PCUSA system — the only reasons to call a legitimate congregational meeting are to deal with the establishment or dissolution of the pastoral relationship; matters related to the pastoral relationship such as changing salary or something similar; the election of officers; the buying, selling, or mortgaging of real property; or matters related to the specifically outlined permissive powers of the congregation. All other areas are under the authority of the congregation's elected representatives — the session. A congregational meeting was out of the question.

Still, in the interest of being responsive to some widely held concerns, I decided that a way around the legal dilemma was to hold an open session meeting on the following Sunday afternoon. (Technically, as an unordained student, I would normally have not been permitted to chair the session, but I had been given authorization to do so some time before and I had been doing it since the beginning of my tenure at Liberty Hill.) Anyone in the congregation would be invited to come to the meeting (which was the regularly scheduled session meeting time) to air their views concerning what had happened. To keep things as orderly as possible in such a charged atmosphere, some ground rules were established: no one would be allowed to speak for more than five minutes at a time; no one person would be allowed to speak twice until all had had the chance to speak once; no individual would be permitted to address another individual — all remarks had to be directed to the session (to prevent any name-calling); and finally, that the session would take no action on what they heard until a later time.

Fortunately, the decision to hold such a meeting proved to be a wise one. Some 25 congregants showed up, about half of the normally active members. (I remember thinking how nice it would be if all these folks would come out to our regular Thursday night Bible study — ha!) People conducted themselves with civility. There was no name-calling or verbal abuse. Thoughts and feelings were aired in a gracious manner. It lasted only about 25 minutes but apparently, a great deal was accomplished. People who had been worried that their concerns had not been heard were satisfied. The complaints suddenly ceased and an air of tranquility seemed to settle over the town. I felt relieved.

As it turned out, the session made some decisions concerning the ongoing situation that day. Once the members of the congregation had dispersed, the elders discussed at length what they had heard and finally concluded that our congregation should have some time to "cool off" before any more joint ventures were considered.

After all, a great deal had happened in a very short time — the joint Christmas program, black participation on Christmas Eve, the worship together on Christmas Day, William Gaither's special music on January 1, the Race Relations Sunday communion service on February 5, Gaither's visit to presbytery that day — all this in a period of just six weeks. They proposed letting their counterparts in the black congregation know of the decision and then to tell them that future joint ventures should be at the behest of the LHUPC since almost all that had occurred so far had been at our instigation.

The following Sunday, February 19, I informed our congregation of the session's decisions. I had hoped that someone other than myself could make the announcement considering the fact that much of the opposition that had arisen had polarized around me. I had wanted our Clerk of Session, Jim Kaylor, to handle the task. Jim had been strongly supportive of our joint congregational efforts since the very beginning — no one had to wonder what his position was. He was not considered as having as personal a stake in the activities as I was, so I thought that he might be the better one to explain our session's decision. Unfortunately, Jim was unavoidably out of town that day and was unable to be in attendance at worship. The ball was back in my court.

I began by offering an apology, not for what had happened to bring the black and white churches together, because I was convinced that what we did was entirely proper. No, the apology was for upsetting so many folks in the process. I was, and still am, genuinely sorry about that. I told them what that little lady had told me about "going too fast," and I confessed that I honestly had not realized just how fast we had been going — it was only after looking at what had been accomplished in only six weeks that I realized what had happened. I told our people how proud I was of them and the way they had handled themselves as brothers and sisters in Christ at the meeting the previous week. Finally, I concluded with an appeal to get on with the ministry of the church and not let our past differences chip away at what God had done among us over the past three years.

I do not remember what I preached that morning but I doubt that it mattered much. People were thinking about what was said before the sermon, not the sermon. On the way out of church that day, there were more than a few tears in people's eyes. The handshakes were especially hearty and the smiles were broad. The tension was gone. We could put our troubles behind us. At least that was the message I read in their faces.

I came home that day with mixed emotions. I was glad that the anger and bitterness had abated, but I was saddened by the fact that, for the most part, these folks would be just as happy never to be confronted by a situation like this again. Even those who had been most ardent in their support seemed to be content to give up the quest. I wondered whether or not perhaps I had led these folks as far as we could go together, whether or not perhaps it was time for me to move on. I had no inkling of feelings from anyone that they were trying to "run me off."

Actually, I got exactly the opposite message — they understood what I had been trying to do, but the time was just not right for it. Virtually everyone would have been startled to know that I was thinking of leaving.

The three years I had been the pastor to the congregation had been extremely fruitful. Attendance at worship had gone from that faithful dozen to an average of 45 to 50. That lakeside ministry during the summers had grown from 35 to 40 a Sunday to an average of 175 each week with several Sundays seeing crowds of well over 200. The little congregation that had been dependent on presbytery for paying its bills had increased its budget by more than 400 percent and was even in a position to extend a call to a full-time pastor if they so chose. The little church that had sold its manse a few years before because it was unable to pay for its upkeep was able to buy another manse and own it debt-free within ninety days after the purchase. The active membership roll had grown by over fifty percent, no mean feat in a no-growth area. Obviously, a great deal had been accomplished in bringing the two village churches into a closer relationship. God had blessed us in many ways. It was traumatic to think of leaving.

My wife and I prayed about the decision just as we had been praying about all that had been going on for those previous six months. We asked for guidance as to whether or not I ought to pursue another call, and it was decided that I should submit my Personal Information Form to denominational headquarters in Atlanta to see what might be the outcome. The answer was swift in arriving. Two weeks after I submitted my form, a pulpit committee from the Oakdale Presbyterian Church in Clover, South Carolina, appeared in the Liberty Hill congregation. Perhaps this was the Lord's way of letting me know that he was calling me to a new field.

The Oakdale pulpit committee knew nothing about the racial situation in Liberty Hill and what had happened between the two little churches there. Had they been aware of it, they might very well have decided not to come. After all, churches generally do not look for controversial pastors. At any rate, the Oakdale folks had come and my wife and I saw a message in that.

Despite the apparent "sign" that it was time for me to move, I still felt a certain reluctance about leaving Liberty Hill with those lakeside services just ten weeks away. Those services were the highlight of the year for that church. I recalled how much difficulty the congregation had had in getting that outdoor pulpit filled prior to their calling me to the task. I was concerned that they might face the same problems again and I was worried about what might happen. Foolish me! If it was indeed the Lord's will that I should move, would he not supply the need at Liberty Hill? Of course! The day after the visit from the pulpit committee, I happened to mention my dilemma to a friend of mine, the Reverend Eugene Rollins, who happened to be the supervisor of a Clinical Pastoral Education unit in which I was involved. It seems that he, too, was beginning to wonder what the future held for him, seeing as how the fellowship under which he was working was soon to come to an end. He was aware of all that had occurred in Liberty Hill, had visited the village along with the rest of our CPE group, and was familiar with the lakeside ministry. When I mentioned my concern, Gene said, "Gee, I'd *love* to do something like that." At that moment I just lifted my eyes to heaven and said, "Thank you, Lord." I knew then that my move was set.

My announcement came as something of a shock to the Liberty Hill congregation. I took pains to let them know that I was only leaving because of God's positive leading and not because of any negatives which might have been involved in our previous experience together. Still, with sadness at the thought of saying goodbye to special friends, but joy at the prospects of what the Lord had in store for us, before spring was out, Gene Rollins had become the pastor of the Liberty Hill Presbyterian Church and the Leiningers had moved to Clover.

Summer Lakeside worship was an important component in the ministry of as small a congregation as Liberty Hill Presbyterian. When David Leininger began at Liberty Hill in June 1981, some 35-40 worshipers gathered from week to week. From the Leininger family collection.

As time went on, the Summer Lakeside Worship services grew in attendance each week, to regular crowds of approximately 175 with several Sundays finding well over 200 attending. From the Leininger family collection.

Chapter 4
Looking Back ... and Forward

As I reflect on the events that took place in Liberty Hill, a passage of scripture comes to mind — the verse in which Jesus asks, "Do you think I have come to give peace on earth? No, I tell you, but rather division" (Luke 12:51 RSV). That scripture took on new life for me as we experienced the incidents that have just been described.

As I mentioned in the Introduction to this little volume, conflict can be a growth process. As Speed Leas says in his excellent book, *Leadership and Conflict*:

> *Conflict increases consciousness, aliveness, and excitement. It wakes folks up, it keeps them on their toes. It enlivens and challenges. Without some challenge and difference organizations and relationships would become dull, constricted, and apathetic — in short, boring. Some anxiety, in other words, facilitates adjustment. It leads to striving; it stimulates learning. Soldiers in the field must have some tension to keep them alert; if they had none, they would let down their guard and their readiness.*[4]

For the churches in Liberty Hill there were indeed challenges prior to the events described in this book, the basic challenges involved in simple survival as viable congregations. But the challenges involved with racial integration in the church most definitely raised the level of excitement. I would say that, no matter what the outcome, that excitement was a healthy thing. People had to take new looks at themselves, their neighbors, and their understanding of the gospel. In some cases, they probably did not much like what they saw — for some, I fervently hope they did not, but at least they looked.

The illustration is often cited concerning the little boy who wishes to help the butterfly escape from its chrysalis — instead of being content to watch that new butterfly struggle to break free, the boy decides to help, allowing the butterfly to get out without much effort. Unfortunately, the butterfly soon dies, lacking the strength it would have developed in the process of leaving the golden sheath. Perhaps we in Liberty Hill were also strengthened in our Christian walk by what happened in our struggles together. I would hope so.

However, one cannot but help trying to reflect in such a way as to see what mistakes were made so as to avoid any repetition of them in the future, to see some ways in which the conflict might have been defused. After all, Jesus also said, "Blessed are the peacemakers ..." (Matthew 5:9a).

My first thought is to say that I am glad I did what I did in trying to get the two churches together. I was, and am, convinced that the goal was one which would glorify God and prove to be a positive witness to the world. Further, I am glad I pursued the goal even in the face of strong opposition. As much as compromise is valuable, there are some things which cannot be compromised without violating one's conscience. Granted, I may have been dreaming the impossible dream, but the greatest advances in the history of humanity came after people did just that. However, beyond the high-sounding rhetoric and self-justification, I realize that I could have done a better job of helping the good folks of Liberty Hill come to share the lofty vision.

My first mistake was in taking too large a role in the project. The attempt at bridging the gap between the black and white Presbyterians in our little village had begun with a resolution proposed by a member of the session. The prospect excited me, so I just took it over. Here was a ministry which could and should have heavily involved the laity of both congregations — the biggest reason that such involvement did not occur was because the minister took virtually all of it on himself. That was a major error, not only in terms of the practical result but theologically, as well.

Another mistake was in not enlisting wider collaboration in our efforts, not only in terms of leadership but in terms of basic participation. In looking back on the situation, I see that there were really very few folks involved in any of the planning. The people in the pews might well have had good insights as to overcoming the roadblocks if anyone [namely me] had asked them. Despite the rather archaic racial attitudes that existed in the minds of some of our folks, the vast majority would have been and were open to change. Their attendance at the special services and encouraging words proved that. If they had been consulted, some of the problems might well have been ameliorated.

Another error on my part was in going too far too fast. I am reminded of a story that was told by a colleague concerning his student days at a well-known military college. Apparently, he was one of the leaders in his barracks and was looked upon by the others to fill that role. One night, he and his buddies felt called upon to raid the students in another barracks across the quad. The plan was to initiate a surprise attack with a fire hose and then gleefully beat a hasty retreat. As my friend tells the story, he and his friends sneaked out of their rooms after lights out and made their way stealthily out of doors. Once outside, however, the fearless leader charged ahead too fast leaving his compatriots too far behind to offer any assistance. The upshot was that my friend got the tar beaten out of him by the ones he was supposed to attack. The lesson? Don't get too far in front of your troops, or they will end up standing and watching while you take your licks.

As I mentioned earlier, I really had no idea how much had occurred in such a short time with the efforts toward putting the two churches together. In the midst of it, the progress seemed to be at a snail's pace. However, in retrospect that was surely not the case. Probably more had been accomplished than anyone would have had a right to expect given the centuries of racial division in our part of the nation. It would probably be exceedingly grandiose of me or anyone else to think that much more should have been hoped for in the same period. The actual fact was that William Gaither and I simply moved too far out in front of our troops. We did not get beaten up because of it, thank God, but we both certainly took our social and psychological licks.

Perhaps a better strategy would have been one similar to that used by mental health professionals in dealing with patients' phobias — desensitization. The phobic is gradually exposed to a greater and greater degree to that which he or she fears with the eventual result [it is hoped] that the fear is either greatly lessened or disappears altogether. If the exposure of one congregation to the other had been taken in more gradual steps, the result might have been different.

My friend's statement about my "going too fast" comes to mind again in this context. As I say, I had no idea just how fast was fast until looking at the events in retrospect. My initial reaction on hearing the phrase from her was a sense of deja vu — the same charge had been leveled against the civil rights activists of the 1960's, but their response was, "Fast? We have been waiting for 100 years!" That kind of thinking was an overreaction on my part. What I was advocating was, I believed, something which should have been done long ago. But the thinking in the community was that things were just fine the way they were. The charge of "going too fast" was perfectly legitimate in this case because something had been sprung on these people which they had never really considered before.

During the course of the events, several colleagues who knew of the situation and of the complaints about "going too fast" suggested that no activity, no speed at all, would have been the only thing that would have satisfied many of the objectors. Perhaps. But, I honestly think that to tar and feather everyone who expressed any reservation with that brush would be unfair. Undoubtedly there were some for whom no steps would have been too many, but those were a small (albeit vocal) minority. As I say, gradual steps would have made better sense.

Another mistake was in not making real "contact" with those who had problems about what was going on. It was not until we held that open session meeting on February 12 — six months after the process had begun — that some of these folks became convinced that they were not simply being trampled in the pastor's stampede toward racial integration and ignored even at that. Had I made more of an effort to draw them out and genuinely listen to their concerns, perhaps the polarization within the congregation could have been avoided.

One avenue of approach, which I did not seriously consider at the time, might have been to bring in some disinterested third party to help mediate the dispute. The third party surely was available to me in my presbytery. Conflict management experts say that a third party can be most valuable in defusing charged situations simply because people will tend to act more like ladies and gentlemen than snorting animals in their presence. Gratefully, I can say that things never deteriorated to the point where I felt I was in a stinking contest with skunks. But a dispassionate third party might have been helpful to both minister and congregation.

I confess that one of the reasons that no third party was called in was my own sense of masculinity — I would handle it. No help needed, thank you! "One plus God is a majority," and all that. That kind of thinking might be appropriate for the John Waynes of this world but not for those who take seriously the "ministry of reconciliation" that Saint Paul talks about (2 Corinthians 5:18).

There is no doubt that I made many more mistakes in this situation than those listed here. Needless to say, I wish I had never made one. The people who were caught up in the struggle were, and are, my friends — brothers and sisters in Christ. I love them. I would have done most anything in the world to have helped them avoid pain, but I am still glad that the process occurred, and equally glad that the good citizens of Liberty Hill, both black and white, were kind to me despite my failings.

Still, despite the difficulties and despite the fact that the ultimate goal was never realized, on balance I would say that the experience was a positive one. My wife insists to this day that the most meaningful worship services she has ever attended were those that were held jointly with the two Liberty Hill churches. Others have commented along the same line.

Lines of communication were opened between the black and white communities. Previously, blacks and whites spoke to each other only within the bounds that the social structure would allow — and certainly not as equals. Now, there was no way to treat one another *except* as equals because one group could have destroyed any opportunity for progress just as much as the other. That can only be thought of as positive. If those communication channels remain open, the benefits to the community beyond the walls of the churches can be remarkable.

The fact that people were indeed forced by events to take a new look at one another in the light of scripture also has to be of great value. Far too often we become complacent in our dealings with one another, content to accept racial, ethnic, or religious stereotypes without holding them up to any examination. That is certainly not conducive to the kind of love of neighbor that Jesus told us to practice.

Over the course of recent years, I have been involved with a couple of encounter/reflection groups with other ministers. Generally, the groups would meet together regularly over a period of months and conclude with some sort of evaluation when it finally came time to disband. Invariably, the evaluations almost always noted that each of the participants had come to new opinions and new appreciation for the other group members during the course of the months spent together — I cannot recall even one instance where no change in the level of appreciation had taken place by the time the group stopped meeting. Perhaps some of that took place between some black and white Presbyterians in Liberty Hill during those months of cooperation. If it did (and I assume it did), that would be positive.

A bit earlier, Jesus' reference to "peacemakers" was mentioned. To be sure, there are any number of ways that exegetes have tried to interpret the Beatitudes. Some would say that they represent an impossible ethic and are not to be thought of as normative for the Christian. Others insist that the ethic is not at all impossible and Christ's words represent an imperative upon all believers. I tend to think that Jesus' words here are not to be thought of as imperatives but rather (playing on the word), BE-ATTITUDES, attitudes that *will be*, once we become genuinely in tune with the mind of Christ, once he is truly Lord of our lives. If we really believe with Saint Paul that "If any one is in Christ, he is a new creation" (2 Corinthians 5:17a RSV), then the result will be a recognition of our spiritual poverty, a mournful attitude toward our sinfulness, a sense of humility, a passionate hunger for the things of God, and so on down the list. That, of course, would include being a "peacemaker."

I have done some wondering about whether or not I would have been more of a peacemaker in Liberty Hill by simply letting well enough (or bad enough, depending on one's point of view) alone. Would I have been more in tune with that BE-ATTITUDE by not stirring up what became a hornet's nest? I do not think so. Allowing the situation to go on unnoticed and untouched would have made me a peace-lover not a peacemaker.

Let me explain. Strange as it may seem at first glance, and despite all the evidence that appears to the contrary, I honestly think that what happened in Liberty Hill fits in with the biblical understanding of peace. Peace in scripture does not merely mean the absence of conflict. The peace of the Old Testament (*shalom*) involves much more: it implies a sense of wholeness, prosperity, and well-being. The peace of the New Testament (*eirene*) comes from a root meaning "linkage," connoting a state of order and coherence. Obviously, an absence of conflict can be a part of those understandings but by no means is it the whole story.

Further, as William Barclay points out in his commentary on this passage:

> ... there is another meaning for this word PEACE. It is a meaning on which the Jewish Rabbis loved to dwell, and it is almost certainly the meaning which Jesus had in His mind. The Jewish Rabbis held that the highest task which a man can perform is to establish RIGHT RELATIONSHIPS between man and man. That is what Jesus means.[5]

Barclay's retranslation of the beatitude reads, "O the bliss of those who produce right relationships between man and man, for they are doing a Godlike work."[6]

If what happened in Liberty Hill is viewed only in terms of the upset that was generated, it could certainly not be called "peacemaking." However, if a larger perspective is taken and the "wholeness" of *shalom* and the "right relationships" of the rabbis of New

Testament days are considered, a wider picture comes into focus. I am convinced that true "wholeness" in Liberty Hill [and in the rest of the nation, for that matter] will only begin to happen when the church and society as a whole develop those right relationships, put aside racial differences and become truly color-blind. If what was done in trying to establish a new relationship between the black and white congregations in that tiny village helped us along that road, then "peacemaking" really did occur.

The question arises as to whether or not I would ever do this sort of thing again, given the results of the attempt in Liberty Hill. My answer would be a qualified, "Yes," but the qualifications are major. I would not do this sort of thing willy-nilly.

The situation in Liberty Hill was unique — two churches of the same denomination within 300 yards of one another separated simply on the basis of race. Without having researched the subject, I would doubt that there are too many communities in which such a configuration exists. However, were a similar circumstance found, I would not hesitate in recommending that a reunion be attempted. I would hope that it might be handled with a bit more cheerful readiness than what was done at Liberty Hill, but I would recommend that an effort be made.

Did I consider such a thing in my next parish? Not at all. Not only were there no black presbyterian congregations within 300 yards, there were none within miles. As a matter of fact, there were not even any black families of any denomination nearby. Our session made it clear that we would welcome worshipers regardless of race to Oakdale, but to be honest, there were no non-whites in the vicinity. It would have been absurd to do anything like what was done in Liberty Hill in Clover. Without an overpowering reason to proceed toward the merger of black and white congregations anywhere, my vote would most likely be, "No," at least not until there was overwhelming support for the idea from both constituencies.

Certainly one consideration in moving forward is the undeniable fact that blacks and whites in America "do church" differently. No, I do not mean worship styles or music or congregational response. Depending on where you might be, you would find those elements interchangeable and not determined by race. Consider simply the place of the church in the life of the community. For example, in predominantly white churches, there is little reference to secular politics (except these days in some very conservative churches who are anxious to support a particular social agenda and who have become, for all intents and purposes, the faithful religious arm of one political party). In fact, many white Christians object vociferously to any mingling of religion and politics from the pulpit. In African-American churches, however, politics and religion would never be thought of as incompatible or as subjects that would not be considered together. In looking at our nation's history, we see that the church was the fertile ground that grew the most powerful and persuasive civil rights leaders, Martin Luther King Jr., Ralph Abernathy, Jesse Jackson, and others. If you put black and white congregations together, which model of "doing church" would be followed?

About a dozen years after our Liberty Hill adventure, I was serving the St. Paul Presbyterian Church in Greensboro, North Carolina, a city with its own interesting racial history. Greensboro was the home of the first lunch counter "sit-in." On February 1, 1960, four young students from North Carolina A & T University came into the downtown Woolworth's Five & Ten and made a few small purchases, saving their receipts to prove they were customers. They then took seats at the whites-only lunch counter and prepared to order. No surprise, they were denied service, but they remained right where they were. The police were called in, but were unable to take any action against the four due to lack of provocation. Woolworth's closed early that day to end the incident, but, as the world knows, that was hardly the end. It was the beginning of a struggle that eventually enmeshed the whole nation. A number of St. Paul members supported the demonstrators that came to town over the ensuing months. The Greensboro Coliseum, a staging area for many of the protests, was less than a mile from the church campus, making St. Paul a handy place to prepare food and drink for the marchers. St. Paul people were heavily involved.

By the mid-1990s, the ugly days of the '60s were just a memory. It would be wonderful to say that all the racial divisions had long since been abandoned, but we know that was not the case. Better, yes, but there was, and is, still a long way to go. Salem Presbytery, the governing body in North Carolina of which St. Paul was a member, was comprised of congregations from both the Northern and Southern streams of the pre-reunion presbyterian church. White congregations, black congregations, a little cross-racial worship by now, but very little. As we say, we "do church" differently.

Salem Presbytery had a task force working on potential sites for developing new congregations. One suggestion was a neighborhood only about a mile and a half from St. Paul for a new African-American congregation. Some folks at St. Paul asked why not encourage the folks who might be drawn to such a new church to come and join us who are already well established and debt-free (always a selling point). As might be imagined, that suggestion never went anywhere. We "do church" differently, after all.

So saying, I do not lose hope. Perhaps there are some situations out there that might be similar to the one in Liberty Hill. If so, and the decision has been made to do some bridge-building, allow me to be so bold as to offer a few suggestions.

1. Go *slowly*! The wise Chinese have the oft-quoted proverb, "A journey of 1,000 miles begins with the first step." There is no reason to "go like sixty" on an issue as delicate as this one. Allow the people to become used to the idea in small stages so as not to overwhelm them with too much too fast.

2. Do not be a Lone Ranger! Activist pastors tend to take more on themselves than is either wise or necessary [a lesson with which I am still struggling]. Delegate responsibilities. Involve as many people in the planning and implementation process as is physically possible.

3. Stay with the troops! There may be any number of folks in the congregations involved who will support and defend the idea of interchurch activity. However, the minister(s) cannot get too far out in front of the leaders of the congregations without losing their backing.

4. Listen! I mean *really* listen — not just with the idea of hearing enough to overcome people's objections, but to hear their pain and fear of change, especially when someone is wanting to change

something as sacrosanct as the church [another lesson I am still trying to learn].

5. Change people's perceptions of problems! With imagination, encourage folks to look at themselves and their situations in a new light, the light of the gospel. Far too often the institutional church has advocated social change without making the biblical basis for such advocacy clear to the people in the pews. The result has been that the church's positions have been roundly ignored. If we would make any improvements in that area, we *must* relate our advocacy to the Word of God that people come to our churches to hear in the first place.

6. Try to equalize the sacrifice! No one group should be asked to make all the concessions. If one group is being asked to give up something dear, then the other should be willing to give up something as well. Without such a spirit of compromise, no lasting relationship is possible. Anyone who is happily married understands.

7. If necessary, ask for help! There is no need to fear bringing in a sensitive third party if the efforts at making change appear to be getting out of hand. The presence of a new element in the mix may very well be able to defuse a volatile situation.

8. *Pray!* Without the intervention of the Holy Spirit, nothing worth doing will really happen anyway. Let both ministers and members remember the source of our power to make or do anything.

As I said in the Introduction, the ending to the struggle in Liberty Hill is not a happy one ... but I do not think it is an unhappy one, either. Both churches continue to operate and indeed are doing well. In fact, the LHUPC has constructed a new building, so worshipers are no longer in danger of an apocalyptic climax to their services. They even have a new name, Messiah Presbyterian Church, so as to avoid the confusion of two similar-sounding names.

Things are okay in Liberty Hill. All that says to me is that the ending has yet to be written, even though my own part in it might be over. As a hopeless romantic and a lover of happy endings, my prayer is that, one day, those two little churches will reunite and will praise God for the opportunity. That will be the happiest ending I can imagine.

Members of both the Liberty Hill Presbyterian and Liberty Hill United Presbyterian Churches gathered for worship on Race Relations Sunday, the first Sunday of February 1984. David Leininger and the Reverend Richard Massey distribute the elements of the celebration of the Lord's Supper. From the Leininger family collection.

Appendix

The sermons on the following pages were preached on the dates indicated in the pulpit of the Liberty Hill Presbyterian Church. The first sermon is one that several of my parishioners requested that I preach to help deal with the tensions that had arisen over several months. The second sermon was delivered to a worship service attended by members of both the black and white congregations in the village in celebration of Race Relations Sunday, 1984.

Appendix

Presented on 1/22/84

A Divided Church

Acts 10:1-36

> *... I now realize how true it is that God does not show favoritism but accepts men from every nation who fear him and do what is right.*
> — Acts 10:34 and 35 (NIV)

That's quite a statement ... indeed, one of the most crucial statements in the entire Bible. Do you believe it? I hope so. It's God's Word.

"I now realize how true it is that God does not show favoritism but accepts men from every nation who fear him and do what is right." We believe it. The question is, "Does it matter?"

Let's look at that. You recall the story. The early church had begun to grow and spread its influence beyond the bounds of Jerusalem. People from all over the world had come under the preaching of the gospel and had been so turned on by the message that thousands were turning to Jesus Christ. But those thousands were, for the most part, Jews. In fact, the early church was *so* Jewish that the Roman authorities considered Christianity nothing more than a *sect* of Judaism. Needless to say, the leaders of the temple did not think that way, but the government did, and that was important. You see, in all the Roman empire, the Jews were about the only people that the government allowed to freely practice their own native religion without interference. Had Christianity *not* been thought of as essentially Jewish, it would certainly not have had the chance to *grow* as it did, and in fact, it might not have ever lasted beyond those first few years. Fortunately for its survival, the early church was almost exclusively Jewish.

Suddenly, one day the leader of that early band, Peter, found himself on a rooftop in the city of Joppa. There he saw a vision that would change the course of history. Three times he saw a great sheet come down from heaven filled with all sorts of animals, reptiles, and birds — things that Jews were not allowed to eat because they weren't kosher. But the voice that accompanied the vision, the voice of God, told Peter to go ahead and eat ... forget about whether they were kosher or not. For Peter, that was a problem. His response to the voice was, "No way, Lord. I have *never* eaten anything impure or unclean." But the message was unavoidable — what GOD says is clean ... is clean. DO IT!

Peter wondered about the meaning of it all, but only for a little while. His rooftop reverie was soon interrupted by some vistors from the home of Cornelius a few miles up the road in Caesarea. Cornelius was a Roman, and a soldier at that — hardly the kind of person that Peter would have *ever* thought of going to visit.

For that matter, for a Jew even to go into the house of a Gentile was thought to make that Jew ceremonially unclean. If you recall, the chief priests and the leaders of the temple refused to go into Pilate's residence even when they had come begging for a rather large favor: a death sentence for Jesus — to have gone into the home of a Gentile like Pilate would have prohibited them from participating in the Passover celebration. Jews could talk to Gentiles on the street ... but a good Jew would not go into a Gentile's house.

Who knows whether Cornelius knew how much of a problem he was presenting to Peter in extending such an invitation? Maybe he did; maybe he didn't. One way or the other, the invitation *was* extended. Apparently, Cornelius had come under the influence of some of this early Christian preaching and wanted to know more about it, social conventions or no. The visitors indicated that their master was really a pretty good fellow despite being a soldier. They even said that some sort of divine messenger had instructed their boss to send specifically for Peter. At any rate, the light suddenly dawned — Peter realized the significance of his rooftop vision and went along without objection.

When he got to Cornelius' house, his Roman host greeted him most enthusiastically. Cornelius even went so far as to *kneel* before Peter in reverent welcome, which took the apostle a little off guard

— Romans just did not kneel before Jews. But Cornelius did, prompting Peter's response: "Stand up. I'm only a man." Then they began to talk as they walked into the house where Cornelius had gathered a number of friends and relatives to hear what Peter might have to say.

It was interesting. The first words out of Peter's mouth were, "You know that under normal circumstances I ought not to be here. It's against our law for a Jew to associate with a Gentile or visit him. But God has shown me that I should not call any man impure or unclean (10:26). There is no one with whom I cannot or should not associate." An amazing admission!

The conversation went on. Peter asked why he had been summoned. Cornelius explained his own vision about asking for Peter to come and then invited the big fisherman to speak to them concerning whatever God had laid on his heart.

Peter stood there, looked around at the people gathered in that large, well-appointed room. He saw the anticipation etched on each of those Gentile faces, and began to speak: "I now realize how true it is that God does not show favoritism but accepts men from every nation who fear him and do what is right."

Wow! For the first time in the history of the church, the most significant barrier to the preaching of the gospel to the entire world was broken ... the barrier of race. But Peter had no choice. If he wanted to be true to the leading of the Lord, that barrier had to be broken. After all, in the last instruction Jesus gave to Peter and his compatriots, he had told them to go and make disciples of *all nations*, and that obviously meant people who were not of the same race. Peter had seen the implications of that instruction in his rooftop vision. The poor man simply had no choice.

Needless to say, Peter got into trouble for it. I mean in the first century or *any* century, you just don't mix and have fellowship with other races without getting into trouble. By the time Peter got back to Jerusalem, word had already preceded him about his indiscretion — news like that travels fast. So the good Jewish brothers jumped him about it. "You went into the house of an uncircumcised man and actually ate with them" (11:3).

That was a very big deal to those folks. You see, in that culture, to sit down at the table with someone was considered the most intimate thing people could do, even more intimate than sex. I confess I don't see how they could make such a mistake, but that's the way they thought. Sitting at table with someone indicated a special bond, a unity, that was not expressed in any other way. That's why Jesus took such heat from the religious types of his day. He actually sat down and ate with tax collectors and prostitutes. That's why the Lord's Supper became such an important element in the life of the church — in a very special way, that sacramental meal showed the special bond between the risen Lord and his followers. Eating together was a very big deal to them.

You find vestiges of that kind of thinking even in our day, and particularly in this part of the country. When my wife was a little girl in Atlanta, her family had a black maid who was considered very dear to them. The only thing that separated them was the family's move to South America when Christie was nine years old. Some years went by, Christie grew up and came back to the States to go to college: Emory University in Atlanta ... a perfect opportunity for her to go and visit her dear old friend. She called Iola and made arrangements to come see her, was invited to dinner and arrived to find the table elegantly set ... with service for one ... for Christie. You see, in Iola's mind, black folks just did not eat with white folks no matter how close they were. Christie tried to change Iola's mind but could not. This was something that just was not done.

That was the situation that Peter faced. The racial barriers in the first century between Jew and Gentile were as high if not higher than the barriers between white and black in twentieth-century America. That meant he had a lot of explaining to do.

To his eternal credit, he was able to manage. He related the story of his vision on the rooftop in Joppa, the visit of the emissaries from Cornelius, the centurion's explanation of the divine message, and finally the outpouring of the Spirit upon the entire company. He had no choice but to conclude that God wanted the racial barriers broken down. His final statement was, "If God gave them the same gift as he gave us, who believed in the Lord Jesus Christ, who was I to think that I could oppose God" (11:17).

To the church's credit, the people listened with an open mind. They, too, were able to see God's leading in this area, and from that time on, Jews and Gentiles were *equally* welcome in the same fellowship, even at the same table.

It's a good thing. Had Peter never seen that vision, had the church never admitted that the gospel was for everyone, regardless of race, I, for one, would have been left out. I'm not Jewish. If Jesus were only for the Jews, I would be left to somehow try to work out my own salvation. I don't know how that would have been possible, but that's what I (and probably most, if not all, of you) would have been faced with.

To be sure, that meeting at which Peter was so eloquent was not the last one ever held on the subject. Racial prejudice is not that easily dispelled. Racial stereotypes are not that easily discarded. People just don't change that willingly. There were problems that would arise now that more than one race was involved in the faith.

Within a short time, people began to note that Jewish Christians and Gentile Christians were not doing things exactly the same way. Those who had come from a Jewish heritage continued to celebrate the feasts of the synagogue — the Gentiles didn't. Those who had grown up Jewish continued to have their sons circumcised on the eighth day, just as their forebears had done for centuries — the Gentiles didn't. Those who came from a Jewish background thought that their ancient laws and dietary rituals — all 613 of them — could not be ignored by followers of Jesus; they must be included as a part of Christianity. The Gentiles didn't believe that at all. That created problems.

Eventually, the church decided to have a summit meeting to resolve the issues. (You'll find the whole story in the fifteenth chapter of Acts.) The leaders met in Jerusalem, heard first from those who felt that *real* Christians had to abide by Jewish laws. Then they heard from Peter who once again said what he had told them after his visit to Cornelius: that God was saving Gentiles in the same way as Jews — by grace through faith in Jesus, not by following certain religious practices. The message was, "God does not show favoritism, but accepts men from every nation who fear him and do what is right." Then Paul and Barnabas stood up and told of God's wonderful work among the Gentiles, of the many who were being saved and of the miraculous things that had happened in that evangelistic outreach. Finally, the leader of the church, James, the Lord's brother, stood up and placed himself and the weight of his office squarely on the side of those who favored racial inclusiveness without restriction. As far as the early church was concerned the matter was finally settled: regardless of race, we are all *one body* ... the body of Christ.

It would be lovely to say that the church has not had to deal with such an issue since then. But, of course, we know all too well that that is not true. There are still divisions in the church based on race. The questions are no longer about whether one group or the other is willing to abide by certain regulations. Now, they are based on not much other than the color of a person's skin. It's true that some will argue that there is more to it than that: that there are genuine cultural differences between the races. (I realize that there are even some who would argue that one race is inherently superior to another, but I won't get into that because there are so few anymore who are really that backward — most intelligent people don't believe that at all.) At any rate, and for whatever reason, the church in modern America is essentially divided along racial lines. And beloved, on the basis of scripture, God's Holy Word, I can come to no other conclusion than such ought not to be ... it is wrong.

Now, I realize that this is an extremely sensitive issue in our congregation right now. Recently, we have joined together with our black brothers and sisters of the Liberty Hill United Presbyterian Church for some joint worship efforts and some people in both congregations have had a good deal of difficulty in dealing with that. Some questions have been raised about why we are are doing anything together at all, what is being planned, and what the long-range future might hold. Let me try to deal with them one at a time.

First of all, why bother? Well, there are several reasons. The most important one I would hope you have already noted: namely that the witness of scripture demands that there be no racial divisions within the body of Christ. The issue that Peter had to deal with in going to the home of Cornelius was not just one of religious practice — it was one of racial prejudice. Jews thought that they were inherently superior as a race to those who were not Jewish. The reason that they would not allow fellowship between Jews and Gentiles was because the Jew did not want to be "contaminated" by some sort of lesser being. That's all there was to it. The message of God's Word in this instance is clearly that those kinds of racial divisions have no place in Christian thinking.

But some would object, "We don't think that way. The only reason we have a black church and a white church in Liberty Hill is because the blacks wanted it that way. It's not our fault." That is true. In 1873, 25 black members of this church asked to be relieved of their membership in this congregation so that they might form another church of their own, the Liberty Hill COLORED Presbyterian Church ... and that request was granted. Was that request prompted only by cultural differences, by a desire to worship in a different way? Hardly! The relationship between the races in the days of Reconstruction in the states of the old Confederacy was abysmal and continued to be abysmal for years after. We all know that. White people and black people were perfectly happy to keep as much distance between them as possible. Fortunately, things are not as abysmal as they used to be, and that in itself can serve as an encouragement to let the church catch up with how far we have come in the rest of our society.

Another reason, of course, is that, as of June 10 of last year, the two Liberty Hill churches are now the same denomination. All that separate us now are 300 yards, a stand of trees, and the fact that we have been separate for many years. When that reunion vote took place in Atlanta, it prompted our Session to unanimously say in a regular meeting on June 12 that, under the circumstances, we feel behooved to attempt to establish some sort of fraternal relationship with the black church. At that time, fellowship between the churches, the only two Christian churches in town, was at such a low ebb that no one in our Session even knew who the officers of that church were or even the name of the minister. Well, that has obviously changed. We do now know who those folks are and, prompted by the action of our two former denominations, we have begun to do some things together — we had those perfectly marvelous Christmas services, and on February 5, Race Relations Sunday, we will come together for another joint service.

Which leads to that second question, "What is being planned?" Well, at the moment, that is it. That is all that is on the calendar. Our Session *has* asked the Session of the black church for a chance to meet together (without the ministers, by the way) to discuss what, if any, possibilities exist for mutual ministry down the road. But, at this point, the Session of the United Presbyterian Church has not yet responded. When they do, and when those discussions are held, both congregations will be carefully informed. But, as I say, at the moment, there are no plans for any intercommunion beyond the first Sunday in February.

What about the long-range future? For those in both congregations who have expressed concern, this has been the big concern. For my part, I have tried to be very open and honest about my feelings on this. I am convinced that a solid understanding of the unity of the body of Christ, a real concern to show the world that the gospel can break down the barriers that people set up between themselves and God and themselves and each other, and a legitimate desire to be good stewards of the resources God has given us, will one day motivate both congregations to become one. I know that that won't happen overnight. The feelings on both sides are so strong that it might not even happen in my lifetime. But I pray that someday, it will take place. That is my feeling.

But, so saying, let me be extremely clear on one thing ... a reunion of these two congregations will never be *forced*. Let me say that again ... a reunion between these two congregations will never be forced. If you missed that, let me say it one more time ... a reunion between these two congregations will never be forced. I hope that is clear now. If these two churches ever get together, it will be because both congregations (and I emphasize *both*) ... both congregations overwhelmingly request it. I cannot force it; this congregation cannot force it; the black congregation cannot force it; the Presbytery will not force it. It will only happen if and when both churches request it.

Now, I realize that there are other questions that might be in some of your minds that I have not answered here simply because of the constraints of time. I would encourage you, if you do have questions or worries or anxieties about all this, that you please talk to me. Don't be content with what, in many cases, turns out to be *misinformation*. If you have questions, ask me — I will answer them to the best of my ability.

I am sure that Peter faced many questions about his vision on the rooftop that were never reflected in scripture. He apparently was able to answer them, and the result was that the church of the first century was able to overcome its racial divisions. With Peter, they were able to say, "God does not show favoritism but accepts men from every nation ... every race ... who fear him and do what is right." My prayer would be that God would provide us with the answers to our questions so that we too might get on with the business of bringing people, black and white, to Jesus Christ.

Let us pray. Father, we confess that the church in our nation *is* divided, even though we know that is contrary to thy Word. Forgive us for being so caught up in our prejudices that we do not see what a sad picture that paints for an unbelieving world. Help us, Lord, to overcome our failings so that we might genuinely show that Christians are one body, and that we might winsomely challenge others to join us under the lordship of Christ. For it is in his name we pray. Amen!

Presented on 2/5/84

The Awakening of Rip Van Winkle

Galatians 3:26-29

I am sure you all know the old story of Rip Van Winkle, that wonderful ne'er-do-well who took off with his dog into the New York woods one day to escape a nagging wife, ended up getting drunk with some mythical characters, and falling asleep for twenty years. Of course, when old Rip finally awoke, things had changed significantly — the wife was gone, his dog was gone, and even his king was gone. Rip had slept right through the American Revolution.[7]

Needless to say, it took a while for Rip to get himself adjusted to some of the changes that had taken place while he had slept, but he finally managed, and as the story went, everyone lived happily ever after.

I am sure you can imagine why Rip Van Winkle comes to mind this morning. If he had gone to sleep somewhere around Liberty Hill twenty years ago and then come into this church today, he would be seeing something that would be tantamount to a new revolution ... the rural South, that historic bastion of racial separation, with both black and white worshiping together today as equals, black and white preparing to come to the Lord's table at the same time. Rip would probably not have dreamed it twenty years ago.

Some did, of course. It was just over twenty years ago that a man stood before a massive throng in the nation's capital and said: "I have a dream today. I have a dream that my four little children will one day live in a nation where they will not be judged by the color of their skin but by the content of their character. I have a dream today ... I have a dream that one day every valley shall be exalted, every hill and mountain shall be made low, the rough places will be made plane, and the crooked places will be made straight, and the glory of the Lord shall be revealed and all flesh shall see it together ... This will be the day when *all* of God's children will be able to sing with new meaning, "My country, 'tis of thee, sweet land of liberty, of thee I sing. Land where my fathers died, land of the pilgrim's pride, from every mountainside, let freedom ring." ... When we let freedom ring, when we let it ring from every village and every hamlet, from every state and every city, we will speed up that day when all of God's children, black men and white men, Jews and Gentiles, Protestants and Catholics, will be able to join hands and sing in the words of that old Negro spiritual, "Free at last! Free at last! Thank God Almighty, we're free at last."[8] Twenty years ago, Martin Luther King dreamed ... but most did not, and I doubt that Rip Van Winkle would have.

But, then again, why should he have been expected to? If a modern-day Rip Van Winkle had fallen asleep twenty years ago and not awakened until today, he would have missed another revolution. He would have fallen asleep in a day when blacks and whites were, in many places, prohibited from eating in the same restaurants, sleeping in the same motels, drinking from the same fountain, even using the same restrooms. To be sure, there had been a good deal of agitation against such practices, but there were no laws on the books at that time forbidding things like that. Rip could have fallen asleep with no idea that, within a matter of months, the law of the land would decree that such discrimination was illegal.

Rip would have fallen asleep in a day when black and white most assuredly would not normally have sat down at worship together, at least not in the South. Rip might have recalled reading of years gone by when that would not have been thought of as such a big deal; after all, in the days before the War between the States, black and white did worship together ... but not as equals, of course. Had he known anything of the history of this church, he might have recalled that black and white did partake of the Lord's Supper here ... but not at the same time. That just was not done.

Now twenty years have passed. Rip awakes. He finds things very different in America. Black people and white people are sitting down together in the same restaurants, riding together in buses; there are no more signs over drinking fountains and restrooms indicating "white only" or "colored only." He would come into our sanctuary this morning and see black and white together in worship, black and white being served Communion from the same trays and at the same time. Quite a shock!

I wonder what Rip Van Winkle would think as he surveyed the scene. I wonder if he would wonder how all this might have happened. Without doing any investigating, he might assume that the churches were where it all started. After all, before he went to sleep twenty years ago, the leaders of virtually all the major Christian denominations were saying that segregation on the basis of race was wrong! Ministers and priests, both black and white, were at the forefront of the drive to end the practice. The cameras of newspapers, magazines, and television networks were always showing pictures of people dressed in clerical collars and nun's habits being dragged off to jail after protest marches. The most visible and charismatic leader of the entire struggle for civil rights was himself a minister of the gospel. Old Rip might come into our church this morning, look around, see the "salt and pepper" complexion of the congregation, and just assume that the church which was the catalyst to all this has been and still is at the forefront of the struggle for "liberty and justice for all."

But suppose he would come to church next week ... or the week after, or the week after that. Having gotten over the initial shock of seeing a nation once completely divided along racial lines now virtually totally integrated, I wonder if he would be shocked to see that the worshipers were once again, either all black or all white, just like the old days. If I were him, I think I would be curious about it.

I might do some investigating and find that, yes, the church was very much involved in the struggle for civil liberty twenty years ago, but the church did not effect the change in American society along that line — it was the federal government. In fact, of all the major institutions of our society, the only one that is *not* integrated in 1984 ... twenty years after all the civil rights legislation was passed ... the only institution that still separates people according to race is the church! Rip would ask around and hear things like "the most segregated hour in America is 11 a.m. Sunday morning." If I were Rip, I think I would be surprised.

I might investigate further and find some very disquieting things about the church. In the twenty years that I slept, those years in which such great strides were made, I would find that membership in the major American churches had undergone a serious decline. On any given Sunday, only about twenty percent of the American population were coming out — millions of people were attending the "church of the inner spring" rather than bothering to get out of bed and come to worship.

There would be all sorts of explanations offered. Some would say that people were staying away precisely because the church was such a champion of things like civil rights — that it had forgotten its mission, the mission to bring men and women to Jesus Christ, not march in protest demonstrations. People wanted to hear the "Old Time Religion," not some new-fangled theology that called for things like racial equality and justice. No wonder people were staying away in droves.

Then others would be heard to say exactly the opposite. They would say that the church had lost its relevance by preaching pie-in-the-sky bye-and-bye while neglecting the poor and needy who were right in its own backyard. They would say that the church had been most vocal in calling for racial equality, but in practice, there was no such thing as equality on a Sunday morning. They would say that the church could talk a good fight, but when it came time for anything to be done, there were all those pious folks just sitting on their hands, ignoring the words of Jesus when he said, "Inasmuch as you have done it unto one of the least of these, my brethren, you have done it unto me." There would be words like those of the black poet, Langston Hughes (1902-1967), who wrote:

> *Listen Christ,*
> *You did all right in your day, I reckon,*
> *But that day's gone now.*
> *They ghosted you up a swell story too,*
> *Called it Bible —*
> *But it's dead now.*[9]

Whatever the reasons offered, Rip Van Winkle would have to conclude that, somehow, the church was not meeting people's needs, neither physical nor spiritual. I wonder what Rip would think.

Sensitive soul that he is (and, if you recall the original Rip Van Winkle, he was very sensitive to the people around him ... at least everybody but his wife), sensitive soul that he is, he would probably sympathize with the quandary of the American church. He would know that there are some things that simply can't be forced; you can't "legislate morality," as they say. Overcoming racial prejudice and bigotry will take time, lots of time. After all, it took lots of time and lots of effort to get us to the place where people would automatically hate someone else for no reason other than the color of their skin.

Rip might even have run into that friend of mine who came to me one day some years ago and told me of a conversation with his six-year-old son. The boy came to him and asked, "Daddy, am I white?" My friend replied, "Yes, son, you're white. Why do you ask?" "Well, Daddy, Eric said I was white and he couldn't play with me anymore." You see, for several years, these two little lads, Eric (who was black) and Josh (who was white) had been fond playmates, not giving any notice at all to the differences in the color of their skin. But now they were getting older, and they had to learn that black and white just did not play together.

No question, we *have* been carefully taught. Despite all we know about the inclusiveness of the gospel, despite reading about God being "no respecter of persons," despite reading that Christians, no matter their color or race, are one as a part of the body of Christ, despite reading that "In Christ, we are a new creation — old things ... old things like racial hatred, old things like fear, old things like bigotry ... old things are passed away — behold, *all* things are become new." Despite all that, the separation continues.

What should be done about it? Some would say nothing at all — don't try to "legislate morality." Let things just take their course naturally. That's an appealing bit of advice. But, unfortunately, not much happens that way. The situation of the churches proves that, had things been left to so-called natural processes, this nation would be as segregated today as it was before our modern-day Rip Van

Winkle went to sleep. Somebody did legislate integration, and because of that, we have made such strides in American society that today a black man can be a legitimate candidate for President of the United States. To let things just take their natural course would never work, because as scripture makes plain, the natural person is a sinful person. "Natural" would just preserve the problem.

How about the other extreme? Why not just force the churches to integrate like the rest of society? That advice might also sound appealing to some. Unfortunately, I don't think it would work any better than letting things go "naturally." There are too many sensitivities that would be trampled in the process, and if we believe that Jesus died for people, not institutions, we have no choice but to be sensitive to what goes on inside people, even the most vile bigot that ever walked. That doesn't mean we have to agree with what we are convinced is a sinful point of view, but it does mean we cannot just run roughshod over the feelings of other folks.

Is there a middle ground that might prove temporarily acceptable while we wait for the Lord to move our hearts to full acceptance of one another? I think there is ... and I think we're marking that ground out right here in Liberty Hill this morning. We have not accepted the easy way, the natural way, the way that is content to do nothing. Nor have we tried to force a full organic union between black and white congregations. What we have done is to make what some might call "a small gesture" by taking a special day, Race Relations Sunday, and joined together for worship ... to acknowledge and celebrate God's goodness to us in the sacrifice of his Son for all who believe, both black and white ... and to gather around the Lord's table as we affirm his continuing nourishing presence with us. Some might say that that's not much, but given the sensitivities of people in modern America, it's really a tremendous first step. You are a part of history this morning.

Does this mean that all our troubles are behind us, that all separation from here on out will cease, that old hurts and animosities will simply disappear? Of course not. What we do here today is not tantamount to the coming of the kingdom, but it is a visible symbol of the fact that Christian people in Liberty Hill really believe that "In Christ, there is neither Jew nor Greek, slave nor free, male nor female." If Paul were writing today, he would include "In Christ, there is neither black nor white." We have not made it all the way yet. We are not yet to the place in Dr. King's dream where all God's children can sing, "Free at last! Free at last!" We can't sing it yet. We still have a long way to go.

What would a modern-day Rip Van Winkle have to say? I don't think there's any question that he would say, "Big change. *Big change!*" But we would have to reply, "No, not such a big change ... but, with the Lord's help, we have made a beginning ... and with his continuing help, the day will come when we will sing,

> *Free at last!*
> *Free at last!*
> *Thank God Almighty,*
> *I'm free at last.*[10]

Let us pray. Father in heaven, we confess that we do not deserve thy mercies. We have not lived the way we ought. We have not even tried to cast off the chains that bind us. We have been too content to just let things go as they have always gone, no matter whether they were right or wrong. Forgive us, Father, and then help us to accept the challenge that our age presents us, the challenge to show the love of Christ, not only in what we say, but also in what we do. For we pray it in his name. Amen!

Endnotes

1. James McBride Dabbs, *Haunted By God* (Richmond: John Knox Press, 1972), p. 177.

2. "Partnership Toward a Culturally Plural Church," Paper and Study Guide, General Assembly Mission Board, Division of National Mission, The Presbyterian Church in the United States (Atlanta, 1979), pp. 6-7.

3. Presbyterian Church (USA), The Constitution of the Presbyterian Church (USA), Part I, The Book of Confessions (New York, The Office of the General Assembly, 1983) The Confession of 1967, 9.44.

4. Speed B. Leas, *Leadership and Conflict, Creative Leadership Series*, Lyle E. Schaller, ed. (Nashville: Abingdon, 1982), p. 109.

5. William Barclay, *Daily Study Bible, The Gospel of Matthew*, Vol. 1, Revised Edition (Philadelphia: Westminster Press, 1975), p. 110.

6. *Ibid.*

7. Washington Irving, "Rip Van Winkle," cited by W. S. Maugham in *Tellers of Tales* (New York: Doubleday, Doran and Co., 1939), pp. 21-35.

8. Martin Luther King Jr., "I Have a Dream," quoted by Clyde E. Fant Jr. and William M. Pinson Jr. in *20 Centuries of Great Preaching*, Vol. 12 (Waco, Texas: Word Books, 1971), pp. 357-358.

9. Langston Hughes, "Goodbye Christ," published in *Negro Worker*, Nov-Dec 1932.

10. King Jr., *op cit.*

www.ingramcontent.com/pod-product-compliance
Lightning Source LLC
Chambersburg PA
CBHW071739040426
42446CB00012B/2396